LONGMAN KEY SKILLS

LEVEL

1+2

COMMUNICATION

Series editor: Barry Smith

Longman

Longman Key Skills

titles available in the series

Application of Number Level 1+2
Application of Number Level 3

Communication Level 1+2
Communication Level 3

Information Technology Level 1+2
Information Technology Level 3

Pearson Education Limited
Edinburgh Gate, Harlow
Essex CM20 2JE, England
and Associated Companies throughout the world

First published 2000

British Library Cataloguing in Publication Data
A catalogue entry for this title is available from the British Library

ISBN 0-582-42484-4

Set by 3 in Sabon and Quay Sans
Printed in Great Britain by Henry Ling Ltd,
at the Dorset Press, Dorchester

Contents

How to use this book

This book helps you obtain the key skill called Communication level 1 or level 2. You will be doing your key skills with your other studies in a school, college or at work. The common combinations are:

Level 1
GCSE and key skills
Part One GNVQ and key skills
Foundation GNVQ and key skills
NVQ1 and key skills

Level 2
GCSE and key skills
Part One GNVQ and key skills
Intermediate GNVQ and key skills
NVQ2 and key skills

A Communication key skill is not asking you to be an expert writer, public speaker or debater. It is about helping you communicate information to other people by writing and talking, and about helping you to understand information and messages written and spoken by other people. The key skill is a simple way of describing all the different skills you use when you speak or listen, read or write.

Communication is often confused with literacy. However, literacy is only about reading and writing; communication includes speaking and listening skills too.

The good news about gaining any of the key skills is that you don't always need to do extra work. The evidence for the key skill is produced while you are doing your normal study and work such as in the classroom, laboratory, workshop, or while working at a job.

Of course there is a certain cunning in knowing which of your work to keep and how to show it, and that's what this book is about. There are special sections for all popular GCSE and GNVQ subjects which tell you exactly what you need to do.

You can use this book in different ways; it depends on what you need. For example, you might not need to read it from the beginning. To get the most out of this book, have a look at the following summary of how it is organised and decide how you can use it best.

The GNVQ Advanced awards are now called **Vocational A-levels**.

From September 2001 GNVQ Foundation and Intermediate awards are likely to be known as **Vocational GCSEs**.

Part 1: The Learning Curve

This part of the book concentrates on what you need to know to get the key skill units. It has useful information about how to participate in discussions, give a short presentation, find and read written information, and create different types of written documents.

Part 2: The Bottom Line

This part of the book tells you what you must do to gain the key skills units. It explains:

- The words and ideas of the key skills
- The difference between level 1 and level 2
- How you can practise the skills
- What must be in your portfolio of evidence

Your collection of evidence or portfolio is the key to getting your key skill. This part of the book tells you how to choose your evidence and get it ready.

Part 3: Opportunities

This part of the book tells you where to find opportunities for evidence in the study or work you are already doing. If you are at school or college, you should look up the pages for your particular subjects at GCSE or GNVQ.

Margin

Look in the margin for simple explanations of important words and ideas and for references to other places in the book where there is useful information.

Part 1: The Learning Curve

This part concentrates on what you need to know to get your key skills qualification. It will show you what you should consider when you:

- Take part in one-to-one discussions.
- Take part in group discussions.
- Give a short talk about a subject.
- Read and understand written information.
- Write documents.

This part is divided into nine sections:

- **Rules for discussions and short talks**
- **Rules for non-verbal communication**
- **Taking part in discussions**
- **Giving a short talk**
- **Reading and using information**
- **Writing documents**
- **Communicating by email**
- **Grammar, punctuation and spelling**

Rules for discussions and short talks

Vocabulary

Vocabulary: a collection of words and phrases.

Your vocabulary is the words you use. When choosing your words, think about your listeners and your readers. You are trying to communicate a message and the key skill is trying to develop your communication skills, so choose words that keep your meaning clear.

Try to convey your meaning using the simplest words you can. Listeners may be reluctant to ask what you mean. And even if they do ask, too many unfamiliar words or too many interruptions will make it hard for people to understand you. Whenever you can, choose a simpler word instead of a complicated word. During informal discussions speak in an everyday voice and use everyday words.

Some language may be very formal and some language may be very informal. Legal documents and medical reports are usually very formal. Emails to your friends and articles in pop magazines may be very informal. But language choices are seldom this clear-cut. There are many kinds of language to cover the range from the most formal to the most informal. The trick is to judge the right amount of formality and to choose your language appropriately.

Always use language everyone can understand. This will often be the language you use in normal conversation. Keep your language simple. Discussions or short talks are not for showing how many big words you know; concentrate on making your points to the audience or the other people in the discussion.

Using jargon

Jargon is the specialist language found in certain jobs or subject areas. Try to avoid using jargon if you can. There will usually be someone who doesn't understand it and perhaps nobody will understand it. These are not good outcomes when your purpose is to communicate clearly. If you do wish to use important technical terms:

- Make sure the terms are crucial to your work
- Introduce them with careful explanations

Using slang

Although slang terms can often be fun, slang is a very informal way of using language. It may not be appropriate in certain circumstances. In less formal conversations, perhaps chatting with friends, slang may be perfectly okay and it can make your approach more personal.

The same is true for vernacular language – words or phrases that come from your home region. Some listeners might not come from your home region and they may find it difficult to understand your vernacular.

Slang and vernacular language are never appropriate in formal writing (business letters, essays, faxes) and in formal discussions and presentations.

Slang: informal language seldom suitable for formal situations.

Getting your tone right

Tone is your attitude towards the subject you are discussing or writing about, or your attitude towards the group you are talking to. Some tones are more appropriate than others for certain groups and purposes. An informal tone and a relaxed manner are usually effective in smaller groups and for brief presentations; a formal tone is better with larger groups and in more serious situations.

Your tone of voice is also a part of communication; for example, you may communicate anger by speaking harshly, or sympathy by speaking softly. An inappropriate voice may create negative feelings in the listener, so practise managing your tone. By speaking a little more quietly than normal, you can sometimes make people listen more attentively.

When you practise a talk, record it on tape. Play it back to hear how you sound; your audience will probably hear something similar. Use your recording to make your talk sound better. Perhaps you need to improve your delivery, perhaps you need to rewrite a section or perhaps you need to cut bits out.

Considering your listeners

Consider how listeners will react to what you say and how you say it. When deciding whether your approach will be appropriate, it helps to know a little about the people you are communicating with. Adapt your voice and your vocabulary accordingly. You've probably heard the phrase, It's not what you say, it's the way that you say it. So before you finalise your approach, consider:

- The people you will be talking to
- The topic you will be discussing

You probably have different ways for talking to your friends and talking to your teachers, talking to people you know and talking to people you don't. Think about how best to talk to the people in your group. Decide whether your subject is serious or light-hearted; this can affect your approach.

Alienate: to make someone feel they are not part of what's going on, perhaps deliberately excluded.

Don't be biased

Be careful not to alienate people during a talk or discussion. Your gender, male or female, can influence the way you think and speak. When you explain concepts or ideas, do not use examples that are familiar to you but which may not be familiar to others. Something familiar to men may not be familiar to women, and vice versa. Try to use examples that will include everybody, and 'everybody' means people of all cultures.

Try not to offend

There is no quicker way to alienate people than by using sexist or racist language. If you remember to include everybody, you should not have this problem. Try to use gender neutral words that include both men and women. Be careful over 'man' and similar words; use 'people' or 'humans'. Watch out for words or phrases generally considered offensive. Check your speech or writing to see how it treats these aspects and be extra careful with any jokes:

- Gender
- Age
- Race
- Disability

Rules for non-verbal communication

Non-verbal communication, i.e. without words, describes your eye contact, body movements, gestures and your overall appearance during your presentation. All these aspects can send messages to your audience and create impressions of what you are like. Some impressions will improve the impact of your presentation and these are the ones you should try to create.

Facial expressions

Your face can reveal a lot about your thoughts and feelings; use it to animate your presentation and bring your words to life:

- Smiling creates a friendly atmosphere, it shows joy and pleasure
- Frowning shows puzzlement, disapproval and concern
- Raised eyebrows indicate surprise

Gestures and body movements

You can use gestures to point things out or to add emphasis. Appropriate gestures will complement your words and make your presentation more interesting and enjoyable. The skill is in choosing them appropriately. Too many gestures, inappropriate gestures or poorly timed gestures may distract your audience. Here are some common gestures and what they mean:

- Head nodding shows interest and attentiveness
- Outfacing palms show openness
- Foot tapping shows impatience
- Neck rubbing shows uncertainty

Using your hands

Using your hands can be another effective way of adding emphasis to what you say. They can help bring your presentation to life but be careful not to let them become a distraction. See how other speakers use their hands and decide which movements were effective in helping them get their points across. If you are not using them in a positive way – to add emphasis or to reinforce the points you make – keep them in a neutral position. Here are some things to try and avoid:

Some non-verbal signs
smiling
frowning
raising eyebrows
nodding
using hands
keeping eye contact
tapping feet
leaning
swaying
fiddling
yawning
dozing

- **Hands in pockets:** this means you can't use them to gesture.
- **Rattling change:** this can be distracting for listeners.
- **Fiddling:** this indicates stress and nervousness; favourite items to fiddle with include rings, necklaces or glasses.

Standing comfortably

There is a lot of talk about the best way to stand, but normally you should have a straight back, your feet apart (about a shoulder's width) and your arms free to move. But above all, be comfortable and have your hands free. Avoid leaning or slouching; don't sway about.

Making eye contact

Practise making eye contact. Try to involve your listeners in what you are saying. Move your gaze around; do not rest on the same few people all the time. By making eye contact with your listeners, you will help them to feel directly involved. Avoid staring into the distance or looking over the heads of your listeners. Maintain eye contact for about a sentence before moving your gaze to somebody else; try not to flit rapidly from person to person. Eye contact helps to keep your listeners alert. It takes practice to develop but is probably the most effective aspect of body language. If you are shy of using it in your presentations, do persevere for the results are well worth the effort.

Taking part in discussions

The key skill will help you learn how to take part in discussions and to participate even when you are not talking. The way you are seated and the way you are listening can create an atmosphere that encourages others to express themselves. You already discuss topics with friends, family and colleagues; this part of the key skill tries to help you develop these abilities so you can take part in discussions with any group of people.

Contributing your ideas

In an ideal group situation everyone would want to participate and everyone would get the chance, all the contributions would be useful and relevant, and the discussion would be a worthwhile experience for everybody. Real discussions are seldom like that, but by working on the key skill you can help them to come closer.

During a discussion you may find that some people talk far more than others, maybe they dominate the exchanges, some people make irrelevant contributions or wander off the point, and some people may say nothing or very little. By thinking about your own role, you already begin to improve the quality of the discussion. You can make the discussion better for you and better for others.

Think about how you behave in the group. Remember that the group will gain more if everyone makes a contribution. This is especially important if the group needs people's reactions to an idea or a set of results. Do not make long speeches; allow others to make contributions and do not interrupt them, otherwise you won't meet the key skill requirements. Nor will you meet them if you just show up and sit quietly.

Types of contribution

There are several ways to make a contribution:

- Making a point
- Expressing an opinion
- Explaining something
- Describing events
- Asking a question

- Answering a question
- Sharing some results

You will be assessed to see if you know how to participate appropriately, e.g. by making the right contribution at the right time or by making contributions that suit the situation. Concentrate on making an appropriate contribution each time you speak. Don't just make one contribution then keep quiet; get involved in the discussion. When you do make a contribution, show that you can adapt what you say to meet the needs of the group and the situation. For example, show you can recognise whether the discussion is formal or informal and act accordingly. Always be polite.

One-to-one discussions

What are one-to-ones?

Taking part in one-to-one discussions is only needed for level 1.

One-to-one discussions are conversations between two people, perhaps between you and a teacher, between you and a customer, or between you and a schoolmate or working colleague. The conversation will be based on an exchange of information between the two people. Each person should have a clear idea of what was said and each person should have gained a better idea of the other's thoughts. This makes it a two-way process. Here are some one-to-one discussions:

- Taking a message
- Getting instructions
- Explaining a problem
- Requesting feedback
- Asking advice

One-to-ones need two-way traffic

Be prepared to give and receive information. Be clear about what you want from the discussion; make a note of your purpose. Now prepare what you want to say; spend a little time thinking about how the other person might receive what you want to say. What questions are they likely to have and how will you answer them? This completes your 'giving' package.

Once you have sorted out the 'giving package', consider how you will use the discussion to get the information you want. Write down your information needs and decide how you will explain them to the other person. What questions will you ask? How will you encourage the other person to give you the information you want? What will you say if you don't understand their reply? This is the start of your 'receiving' package.

This type of forward planning can work with face-to-face discussions and with telephone conversations. It can help to ensure that you get the information you need and the other person gets the information they need.

In a work situation you may not know what the other person will ask.

Respond appropriately by answering their question or by helping them to find someone who can. Make sure you understand their question and make sure they understand your answer.

Useful techniques for one-to-ones

Face-to-face meetings

Be clear about the information you are able to give and the information you want to receive. Here are some helpful techniques:

- Notes can be a useful way of reminding yourself about what you need to say or ask. You should certainly take notes when you are told important information.
- Repeat your main points and check that they have been understood.
- Check you have understood key points by repeating them back.
- Prepare your questions, especially the follow-up questions you may need to ask if your first question doesn't answer everything.
- Prepare answers to the other person's possible follow-up questions.
- Use appropriate tones of voice, body language, facial expressions and, most importantly, eye contact.
- Look at the person you are speaking to; this helps to show you are listening and allows you to give and receive extra feedback on whether you understand each other.

Telephone discussions and conversations

Most of the points about face-to-face meetings also apply on the telephone; but with no body language or eye contact, listeners will form opinions from your manner and tone of voice, so they become much more important. Here are some other things to consider:

- Write down your points in a logical order
- Speak slowly and clearly
- Be polite and friendly
- Repeat your main points over to the listener
- Repeat back the main points from the teller
- A smile on your face can be heard in your voice

The group situation

Create a discussion group from people you are comfortable with and discuss a topic that will interest the group. During the discussion take brief notes of key points, important decisions and who said what. They may help you to make your contribution. If you attribute an idea or comment to someone, make sure you name the right person. Done well it can be a compliment, but done badly it can lead to unnecessary arguments. The notes you take can provide a useful record of your involvement.

Perhaps begin by jotting down the names of the people taking part or even a rough seating arrangement. This will help you to identify who's

Taking part in group discussions is needed for level 1 and level 2.

who. Keep your notes brief; spend most of your time looking at the speakers not at your notepad. Eye contact is important.

Always

- Be aware of your surroundings
- Be aware of other group members
- Be polite and supportive
- Speak clearly when you contribute
- Wait for people to finish speaking

Never

- Shout or raise your voice
- Be rude or angry
- Dominate the discussion
- Decline to participate

GET INVOLVED IN DISCUSSIONS

Try to get involved in discussions with small groups of people, perhaps between 4 and 8, and focus on shared interests. A shared interest might be an assignment or investigation you are all working on, or it might be an issue that interests you all. Topics that make for good discussions normally involve problems that need solving, issues that need to be debated or resolved, and questions that must be answered.

Listening

Even when you are not talking, there's still work to be done.

The point of a discussion is to exchange information and ideas with others; this means giving and receiving. The simplest way to show someone that you are listening is to look at them. You can also jot down the points they make, especially those you think are important.

There is a difference between hearing someone's voice and listening to what they are saying. It can be very off-putting to realise that people are not listening. The speaker sees the signs in glazed eyeballs, stifled yawns and perhaps even more obvious displays. And the message comes across: I'm not interested in what you're saying; I'm only interested when I'm talking. So be attentive and make sure that you really do listen to people.

Being attentive is what typifies a good listener. It means using different listening techniques to let others know you are taking an interest in what is being said. The following table shows a range of techniques to indicate you are paying attention, and you may be surprised how effective they are. But just imagine how you would feel if no one looked at you when you spoke. In fact, not looking at someone can be a sign that you aren't impressed by what they have to say.

Listening technique	How to use it
Facial expressions	Give clues on how you are receiving someone Puzzled looks can encourage them to explain
Body movements	Nodding in agreement can be encouraging Shaking your head is good if you time it well Tilting your head shows you are listening Crossed arms look defensive Open palms add emphasis
Asking questions	Base your questions on what people have said What did you mean when you said . . . ? You mentioned . . . . Can you explain it to me?
Verbal encouragement	Offer an occasional word or nod of approval Try something like yip, uh huh, mmm

Primary school rule
You have two ears and one mouth, so listen twice as much as you talk.

AN EXPERIMENT ON VERBAL ENCOURAGEMENT

Try this exercise to investigate the importance that speakers attach to verbal encouragement or reassurance. When a chatty person telephones you and starts to tell you something at length, make sure you keep quiet and say nothing. Don't even grunt or say yeh; just say nothing at all. See what kind of reaction you get. They will probably find it disconcerting and keep checking that you are there. Most telephone speakers expect their listeners to give them an occasional sound of reassurance.

When you are not under the spotlight and are in a normal conversation with a friend or a family member, you are probably highly accomplished at using these gestures. What you might need to practise is your ability to use them during your key skills assessment without being shy or inhibited.

Understanding the facts

To test that you understand what someone has told you, repeat it back to them in your own words. It should then be clear that you have understood what was said; if you haven't understood, the other person should be able to re-explain. You can also use follow-up questions to check your understanding, or simply ask the other person to explain the whole thing in a different way.

Listening between the lines

People often talk about reading between the lines; this means recognising what a writer is really trying to tell you. Listening between the lines means recognising what a speaker is really trying to tell you. Try to figure out their intentions by asking yourself these questions:

- What are they trying to do?
- What do they want to find out?
- What is their purpose?

The most obvious way to get the answers is to listen to what they are saying; this may reveal a lot about their purpose but perhaps not everything. You may be able to get a fuller picture by considering the speaker's body language, their tone of voice and their choice of words. Use what you know about your own body language, etc., to predict what theirs might be saying. Once you understand a little more about listening between the lines, you can begin to detect people's signals quite accurately.

It is a useful ability to interpret and understand a speaker's intentions. For example, if you detect a speaker is nervous then you can help to put them at ease. If a speaker has not been clear but you are still able to spot their purpose, you can help them to achieve it and perhaps save them embarrassment or inconvenience.

If someone does ask you a question that seems a little vague or unclear, try to answer it politely and check with them to discover their intention. Be tactful, don't embarrass them or put them on the spot. Be supportive and help them out.

Always be polite even if a person appears to be acting mischievously or with bad intentions. By being polite and courteous you are showing that you can detect their intentions but you are not willing to play their game.

HOW TO PRACTISE LISTENING BETWEEN THE LINES

Watch speakers on television, especially MPs appearing on the news. See what you can learn about their purpose or their intentions by looking at the language they use and the non-verbal signals they give out. You could also watch teachers or friends in a discussion to see how they interact.

Asking questions and responding to others

Questions and answers

The key skill is looking for two things:

- Whether you can listen and respond appropriately
- Whether you can use questions to encourage others

It does not expect you to have all the answers nor is it trying to see how cleverly you can avoid answering people. If you don't know something, there are three things you can do:

- Admit that you don't know
- Say how you could find out
- Ask if anyone else knows

It is important to realise the limits of your knowledge, and it is often the first step towards expanding them.

When you do answer a question, there are three things to remember:

- Use the questioner's name in your answer
- Repeat the question before you give the answer
- Do not humiliate anyone during your answer

Repeating the question before giving the answer is especially helpful in large groups where some people may not have heard it. It also gives you a moment to prepare your answer. It is unkind to humiliate people, even if they have asked a silly or irrelevant question; it is much more helpful to be positive and give them a straight answer.

Someone may have already asked a question very similar to one you've prepared; unless you have a good reason, don't ask yours as well. The key skill is looking for appropriate contributions, and needless questions will rarely count as appropriate.

Type of question	Purpose	Examples
Open	To open up discussion, to obtain an explanation or to go beyond a yes/no answer	Why do you think ...? How would you ...? What do you think about ...?
Closed	To get a short or yes/no answer	When are you going to ...? Is this a good or bad ...?
Follow-up	To pursue a point or to get more information	What did you mean when you said ...?

Helping others participate

Creating a good atmosphere

One of the best ways to encourage others to participate is to create the right atmosphere for a discussion. This means making sure that people don't feel intimidated or worried about participating. Play your part in helping to make the atmosphere light and friendly, receptive and non-threatening. Give encouragement to other people's ideas, comments and suggestions.

Sensitivity

The key skill is trying to help you develop an awareness of others and the ability to show sensitivity when you participate in discussions. You can empathise with people by imagining what they might be thinking or feeling; try to see the discussion from their point of view. You may be able to help people feel more comfortable by using some of the techniques mentioned earlier.

How you behave and the tone of your voice can affect the ways others will react or participate. When the topic is serious, don't be flippant. Be positive, supportive and friendly, and choose an appropriate tone of voice

Receptive: willing to listen to new ideas or suggestions

See also: **Rules for non-verbal communication**, page 5.

Empathy: showing you understand how others are feeling.

that will help to create a good atmosphere and encourage others to feel confident and able to take part.

Helping to include others

You are expected to show that you can help others to take part in the discussion. If someone is finding it difficult to make a contribution because they can't seem to get the group's attention, then invite them to make their point. Create an opening for them and invite them to speak. But don't turn the spotlight on someone who won't be comfortable with this attention.

You can ask follow-up questions to help someone get more involved in the group discussion. Perhaps ask them to elaborate or explain some of their comments. Ask them in a supportive way, showing that you are interested. But be sure the person actually wants to make further contributions, otherwise you may increase their anxiety. Try to judge if the person would be comfortable making further contributions, if you think they would not then don't ask.

Giving a short talk

Perhaps you are dreading the moment when you have to give a short talk, but it needn't be too daunting. Let's begin with what *isn't* required of you:

- You are not expected to talk for a long time
- Your talk need not be on something complicated
- You do not have to be a stand-up comedian
- Your audience need not be a large crowd

Here's what is required of you:

- Give a short talk to a group of people and do it effectively
- Adapt your content and delivery to suit your audience and your subject
- Use some sort of image during your talk

You can talk about almost anything you want to. Perhaps choose a subject that interests you or can help you with your other courses. Here are some suggestions:

- Hobbies or interests you have
- Results of some research you did
- A matter where you hold a strong opinion
- A topic from a course you are studying

If you have another idea for a talk, ask your teacher. They will be able to tell you whether or not it is appropriate. The key skill wants you to talk about something straightforward, so you needn't discuss anything really complicated or difficult.

Using an image

The image is a visual aid for your talk. Use it to help explain a point to your audience. Here are some suggestions. Check any other ideas with your teacher.

- Model
- Picture
- Sketch
- Technical drawing
- Diagram
- Map
- Photograph
- OHT

OHTs and OHPs
OHTs are overhead transparencies.
OHPs are overhead projectors.
OHPs project OHTs onto a screen.

How long is a short talk?

The key skill requirements don't actually give a time in minutes, they just say 'a short talk'. Don't worry about the exact length; concentrate on demonstrating your communication skills. If you put together an introduction, a few main points and a conclusion, your talk should be quite long enough. Using your visual aid will also take up time.

How many listeners do I need?

The key skill requirements don't give a specific number, but it needn't be very many. The nature of your audience, including its size, will probably depend on the subject of your talk. Choose your subject first, then think about your audience. It is not always easier to give a talk to a small audience than to a large audience. But when you are developing your skills, it probably makes sense to start with small audiences.

Preparing your talk

Reasons to talk and listen

Try to avoid doing a presentation on something just for the sake of getting this part of the key skill evidence. Identify a topic that could be presented as part of another course. This could be part of a GNVQ unit or part of your GCSE work. Why not use the presentation as an opportunity to revise something that might come up in an examination or assessment. This may also give your audience a reason to listen. Another good subject for a talk is one of your hobbies or interests. For example, you could speak to a school or college club or a meeting. People who share your interest will be keen to listen to you.

How to use notes

You needn't memorise the whole of your talk and you mustn't read it like an essay. You will need to work from notes that help to jog your memory but leave you free to make eye contact, use visual aids and do all the other things that go to keep an audience interested.

Some people like to have notes on paper, some use cards and some use paper copies of OHTs or computer screens. Experiment to see what suits you best. Here are a few general tips:

- Write or type your notes on one side only
- Use large letters that can be read at a glance
- Number each card or page in case you drop them
- Put each main point on a separate card or paper
- Leave lots of space for last-minute changes
- Don't make too many last-minute changes
- Carry a spare set of notes

Keep your notes clear; don't crowd your pages. Highlight key words or concepts to draw attention to them. Don't highlight too much or you will defeat its purpose. Maybe have a checklist of things to do before you start your talk:

- OHP in focus
- OHTs in order
- Notes in order

Adapting your language and delivery

Record your method

Your method is how you adapt your talk and the message you want to give to your audience. It includes strategies, visual aids, language and how you organise your talk. It is everything you think will work well for the people listening to you. Make notes about your method as evidence for your portfolio. Writing about your method helps to set a context for your talk; it explains your intentions and gives an insight into your thought processes.

Vary your pitch

The pitch of your voice is also important. Vary it to suit what you are saying and how you feel about it. Varying your pitch is an important way to keep the audience interested. Think about the way people vary their pitch when reading stories to young children. It can be quite dull to listen to a voice that hardly varies at all.

Structure and organisation

Organising what you say

Try to draft your presentation using a computer. This will let you edit, save and spellcheck your work. It can help you change notes into OHTs or computer screens. You can also create documents to record your thoughts on the audience and the techniques that you tried.

When you work on the structure, think about what you want to say, when you want to say it and how you want to express it. Make your structure easy for your audience to follow. A good structure is to have a beginning, a middle and an end.

Beginning

You need a way to introduce your subject to your listeners. Here are some questions that may be in their minds:

- Who is giving the talk?
- What are they going to say?
- How long will it last?
- Should I take notes?

Use the introduction to set the scene for your talk. Explain what you will be covering and give your audience a reason to be interested.

Good things for an introduction

- Say that you're happy to be speaking
- Make a connection with the audience
- Give listeners a reason to be interested
- Capture attention with an intriguing title, phrase or question

Bad things for an introduction

- Organise items you should have prepared earlier
- Admit you're not prepared or feel nervous
- Try to be too clever and start with a joke
- Use people's names and get them wrong

Middle

The risk of losing your audience is usually greatest during the middle of your talk. This is where you need to use techniques such as eye contact to hold people's attention. If you are giving information, the middle is where you deliver most of your facts. If you are making a case, the middle is where you present most of your arguments. Do not overload your audience; restrict yourself to three or four main items and always say when you are moving from one item to the next.

Organising the middle as a list

Most audiences can easily follow a list of points. You could write the points on an OHT, cover it with a sheet of paper and reveal one at a time. Use other OHTs to supply more detail. Tell your audience which points are more important than others. Say when you are moving on to the next point and tell the audience when you have covered the final point.

Organising the middle by problem then solution

Start by describing a problem, explain the issues involved then propose a possible solution. This is particularly well suited to design briefs and activities presented as a challenge. Organise the issues into a logical sequence then make sure they fit with the beginning and the end. One way to produce a logical sequence is to start with the most important issue and work through to the least important issue.

End

When you began your talk, you probably said how long it would last or gave the time it would finish. Stick to your promise. Indicate you are near the end by using recognised phrases. Recap your main points, provide a brief conclusion and then stop. Never tell the audience you are coming to the end and then launch into a new set of points; this really upsets people. Listeners tend to remember the beginning and end of a talk more clearly than the middle, so try to have an interesting start and a satisfying finish.

Structure in a nutshell

- Repeat important facts and key points
- Use clear notes and keep them brief
- Arrange your points in a logical order
- Do not read your notes like an essay
- Glance at keywords to jog your memory
- Use simple words in short sentences
- Speak clearly and go at a steady pace

Using visual aids

Visual aids, such as OHTs and flip charts, can raise your confidence. They help you to pace your talk and remind you what you want to say. They give the audience something else to look at. The most common visual aids are overhead transparencies (OHTs), flip charts and computer presentations.

Some computer packages may have templates to help you with OHTs.

Using OHTs

OHTs can guide you through a talk and may be easier to use than your notes. Try to create them on a computer. Lay out each page using a word processing package, print them onto paper then photocopy them onto transparencies. Make them look neat and professional:

- Use letters that are large enough to read
- Use wide margins and plenty of space
- Break up text with informative headings
- Number each transparency in case you drop them

Decide on the important information and restrict yourself to that:

- Don't put too much information on each transparency
- Don't get carried away when designing your layouts
- Don't use too much bold or italics
- Only put the important information on the OHT and only highlight the *really* important information

Some speakers distribute paper copies of their transparencies before the talk begins. This may cut down on note taking and it allows you to con-

tinue if the projector fails. But it does mean that some people may read your handouts instead of listening to you. This takes away some control you have over the talk and makes it more difficult to surprise people. One way to overcome this is to distribute your handouts at the end.

USING AN OVERHEAD PROJECTOR

- Check that the OHP is ready and in order
- Have a back-up plan in case of technical failure (e.g. if the bulb fails)
- Try out one of your OHTs on the projector to check it is correctly focused
- Point at the OHT not the projected image – this keeps you facing the group
- Keep away from the OHP cable to avoid tripping up

Charts, diagrams and graphs

Charts, graphs and diagrams are great for numerical information or statistics. They can be used on OHTs or flip charts. You can also use tables as long as they are not too big. Tables with many entries may be okay to read in books and journals, even on computer screens, but they rarely work well as part of a talk. Only use statistics when they make your points clearer; don't use them to hide any gaps in your argument or weaknesses in your preparation. Here are some tips:

- Keep your graphs and diagrams simple and clear
- Give them a title and label the important features
- Choose appropriate scales to illustrate your points
- Use them sparingly; don't overwhelm your audience

Flip charts

Often best with small groups, flip charts work well when your talk covers clearly defined stages. Put each stage on a separate sheet, then as the talk moves from stage to stage, you can flip your chart from sheet to sheet. Each time you flip, give the chart a tilt to draw people's attention. Some speakers put full details on the flip chart before they begin the talk; other speakers set up the headings and write in more information as they go along. You can follow most of the rules for OHTs and here are some that are specific to flip charts:

- Write clearly in letters big enough to read
- Do not put too many words on each sheet
- Use pens that have dark colours, e.g. black
- Don't talk to the chart, talk to the audience
- Give people time to read what you have written
- Put the pen down after writing; don't fiddle

Handouts

Handouts save a lot of note taking for the audience and may help you to guide people through your material. But, almost certainly, some people will prefer to read the handouts instead of listening to you. One way around this is to distribute them at the end. Always tell the audience at the beginning if this is what you are going to do. Long handouts or detailed material could be distributed at the end of your talk, but a brief summary of the structure is probably better given out at the start.

Presenting work using a computer

Computers can help you to show your work to other people, such as presenting the results of a project. Word processor, spreadsheet and graphics programs give you plenty of choices for making your work look good.

Whichever method you use to present your work, it is important to make a good impression. Here are some things you can do to check and improve your work:

- Check that the content is relevant – don't use it just because you have it.
- Select the important information and make sure it stands out.
- Put lots of space between items.
- Beware of using too many fancy effects.
- Use a spellchecker then use a human being.
- Ask other people what they think.

Presentation programs

Specialised programs, e.g. PowerPoint, are designed to help you make materials for presentations and then to run the presentations. You can use presentation programs for the following purposes:

- Create OHTs or slides
- Store OHTs and slides
- Run a slide show from a computer
- Fade in and out between slides
- Print paper copies of all slides
- Print summaries of slides

Most presentation programs work in the same general way and have the following basic features:

- **Design options** allow you to choose different styles of ready-made slide plus ways of laying out information and graphics.
- **Notes provide** information to go with the slides.
- **Clip art** can be added along with other pictures.
- **Graphs and charts** can be imported from other packages.
- **Edit commands** allow work to be changed using undo, cut, paste and copy.

Typical presentation slide combining text and graphics

- **View** generates different types of slide, summaries, speaker notes and handout notes.
- **Slide show** allows you to show the slides full-size on the computer screen or on a projector screen; there is the option to add timing and let the slide show run automatically.
- **Slide effects** include special effects as slides change and added sound effects.

Presentation software is great for making OHTs. Some packages have a wizard for getting started and a spellchecker for the finishing touches. But though they are brilliant, they cannot write your talk or deliver it to your audience. Think of them as the icing on the cake. Read the user guide carefully and become familiar with the software. Use it wisely; you are giving a talk not staging a light show.

Wizard: a help feature in a software package that makes complex tasks easier for beginners.

READING SOFTWARE MANUALS AND USER GUIDES

Reading and understanding a software manual or user guide (while creating your OHTs) might enable you to generate evidence for the key skill requirement on reading and summarising information.

Reading and using information

There are many reasons why we read:

- To obtain information
- To learn how to do something
- To check a text is accurate
- For recreation and pleasure

To read effectively at this level, you should be able to collect information from a range of text-based sources and images such as:

- Charts, tables and graphs
- Diagrams, maps and plans
- Drawings, pictures and sketches
- Photographs and illustrations
- Signs and symbols

The most important thing is to understand what you are reading. Short passages are usually quite easy to comprehend but longer works require greater concentration, especially if you have to remember several ideas at once. Take notes as you go along; they will help to jog your memory.

You are expected to obtain information from straightforward documents and images. At level 2 you must identify the sources for yourself and you must summarise the information you will use.

Finding and using sources

Selecting appropriate material

A lot of your information will probably come from text, but some may come from emails, telephone conversations or face-to-face discussions. Here are the main text-based sources:

- Textbooks and reference books
- Directories and dictionaries
- Letters, memos and emails
- Newspapers and magazines
- Teletext pages, e.g. Ceefax
- Websites on the Internet
- CD-ROM encyclopedias, etc.

- Exhibition guides and catalogues
- Library collections and museums
- Posters, leaflets and other publicity
- Manufacturers' catalogues and data

Be clear about why you are gathering information. Perhaps you wish to find out about a particular writer. Where do you start? You could ask other people to give you some suggestions. They may give you a book list or suggest somewhere to visit.

Libraries

A library contains a large number of information sources. To help you find what you want, it is organised into different subject areas. Small libraries may use a small number of broad categories (for example: art, literature and science); big libraries may use a large number of narrow categories (for example: accounting, biology, computing, through to zoology). You can identify the material you want by looking at the library's catalogue. Some libraries still keep their catalogue on small index cards held in drawers and arranged in alphabetical order. However, most now store this information electronically for access by computer.

When you find an item that interests you, make a note of its classification number; this tells you where to find it on the library shelves. The library shelves usually have clear numbers and each aisle often has a big sign, but it is easy to miss an alcove tucked around a corner. If you need assistance, ask the library staff. Perhaps the library does not have what you want, but it can usually be obtained from another library; the library staff can also help with that.

Basic details for books and periodicals

When searching for information in books and articles, it is important to have the following details:

- Title of book, journal, newspaper or magazine
- Name of author, editor, contributor or columnist
- Publication date, volume number and pages
- Name of publisher

How to ask for help

You will need to use your speaking and listening skills to help you obtain the information you need. These skills are just as important as your ability to search for and find information from written sources. When asking people to help you find written information you should always:

- Be clear about the printed works you are looking for
- Speak clearly and audibly; don't speak too quickly
- Do not get too close to people; watch non-verbal signs
- Wait until people are free to help you; don't interrupt
- Be polite and courteous; use a respectful tone of voice
- Note names and numbers so you can contact people again
- Thank people for giving you help

Using the Internet

When computers are connected together they make a network, such as you might get in a school or college. On a larger scale you can have a wide area network (WAN), such as when cash dispensers in the streets are linked to large computers in the banks.

The Internet is a system which allows any computer in the world to join together a system of link-ups. At home we usually link to the Internet via our phone line but larger computers in the Internet are connected by high-speed telecommunication links which use cable and satellite.

The Internet can be used in different ways but the two main uses for most people are **email**, described in a later section, and the **Web**. The Web is part of the Internet where organisations or people have pages of text and pictures. From these pages you find things, buy things or jump to other pages. You get directly to a **website** by entering the address into your browser. Website addresses often look like this:

www.name.com

www.name.co.uk

Looking up websites

To use the Internet you subscribe to an **internet service provider** (ISP) who has a computer which links you to the Web. You connect your computer to your ISP using a modem and a special phone number. Your computer will have an icon for dial-up connections. Click on this icon to connect to the Internet; you may need to enter a password before the modem begins to dial. At work, college or school your computers may be permanently connected to the Internet.

When you're online to the Web you will use a **browser**, such as **Microsoft Explorer** or **Netscape Navigator**. The browser is a computer program which displays webpages.

Using a browser

All types of browser work in a similar manner and have a banner along the top of the screen where you click to give commands. The main commands are explained in the following table.

Icon	Effect when clicked
Address or Go to	Allows you to enter the address or name of a website that you want
Back	Takes you back to the webpage you just visited
Forward	Moves you forward to a webpage you just came from
Stop	Stops loading the current page
Refresh or Reload	Loads a new version of the current page; useful when a page is incomplete or often updated

Networks
local area network (LAN)
wide area network (WAN)
World Wide Web (WWW)

Some ISPs
AOL
BT Internet
Bun
Claranet
Compuserve
Freeserve
Virgin Net

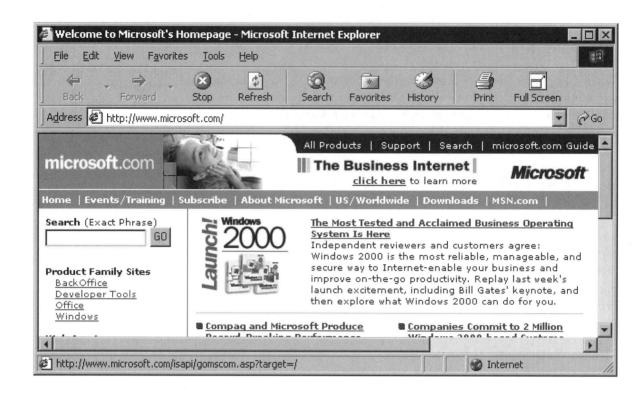

Internet browsers: Internet Explorer and Netscape

Icon	Effect when clicked
Home	Goes to the page seen when your browser opens; this can be changed to whatever you want
Search	Begins options which search by keyword
Favourites or Bookmarks	Drops down a list of favourite websites you have marked in the past
Mail	Connects to email
History	Gives a list of the websites you have visited in past days or weeks
Mail	Opens the options for using email
Print	Prints out the webpage shown on-screen

The most important thing is to get started using the blank line near the top of the screen called **Address** or **Go to.** Suppose you want to see the website with address www.bbb.co.uk:

Most general website addresses start with **www**.

- Type it into the address box of your browser.
- Check you have typed it correctly.
- Press the **Enter** key
- Wait for the webpage to download into your computer.

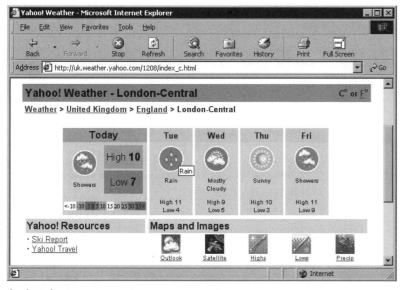

Typical Web page

STOP BUTTON

If a download is slow because it has many images, click the **Stop** button once the text is on-screen. If you want to see an image then right-click on the blank image. Also, use the **Stop** button if a connection is very slow; you can try again at a less busy time.

Searching the Internet

The Internet joins you to the information held by thousands of computers worldwide, so it is the largest database in the world. Somewhere on the Internet are websites with answers to your questions, but they have to be found. You can reach this information in the following two ways:

- **Go directly** because you know the website address.
- **Use a search engine** to trawl the net for relevant websites.

Popular search engines
AltaVista
AskJeeves
Excite
Google
HotBot
Infoseek
Lycos
MSN Search
Northern Light
Yahoo

Search engines

Some well-known search engines are described in the following table. Some of the engines let you enter your question in general language. Others work better if you use the tricks for advanced searches.

Search engine and address	Notes
AskJeeves **www.ask.co.uk**	Allows you to ask questions in plain English, although some of the answers may be too general
MSN Search **www.search.msn.com**	Good site for beginners and good links to other information
Yahoo **www.yahoo.co.uk**	Can be browsed by categories or can be searched by keyword
AltaVista **www.altavista.com**	Indexes more webpages than many engines. Also has advanced search option to focus your seach

Two typical search engines (AskJeeves and AltaVista)

Advanced searches

Some types of search involve the logic of combinations. This is particularly true when searching huge databases like the Internet. For example, searching for 'spice girls' could bring you thousands of references for 'spice' as in cooking and 'girls' as in girls.

But if you want to find the pop group Spice Girls then you can link the two words together by using AND. This will force the search engine to look for references where the words are joined together. Here is how you search for websites about blue whales.

Extra search conditions (word or symbol)	Possible effect
AND +	Will find references which include the word *blue* joined with the word *whales*. This condition will probably find the references to the particular type of whale
OR −	Will find references which include either the word *blue* or the word *whales*. This condition will find thousands of references you don't want

Effective reading

Three types of writing

When you look at a piece of writing, decide which of these three types it belongs to. Consider why it was written and investigate how it could be biased.

- **Writing with a personal opinion** is called subjective writing; it includes fiction, personal accounts or records, advertising, publicity and promotional material.
- **Writing with a strict purpose** is called functional writing; it includes reference books, directories, instruction manuals, handbooks and technical documents
- **Writing with no personal opinion** is called objective writing; it includes official reports, guidance material and research findings.

Always find out about the context, purpose and intended readership of your sources of information and text. This will help you understand the writer's intention.

Skimming and scanning

Skimming and scanning are two techniques that help you find the information you need quickly without having to read the whole text. They can also help you find time to use more sources of information in your search.

Both help you find the relevant information you need so you can concentrate on reading only what is important to you.

Once you have identified the author or subject areas you are interested in you can begin to look for the information you need. The more specific your search, the easier it will be to skim text for the relevant headings.

Skim to locate information quickly

Skimming can help you get a quick, general idea of the content of a book, magazine or report and will give you important clues about where the information you need might be found.

The first thing to look at when opening a book is the contents list at the front (usually right after the title page). It contains the headings of the main sections of the book, which help you find your way through it. However, if there is something very specific you wish to search for, the index, found at the back of the book, will be more helpful.

Generally speaking, skimming will help you get an impression of a text and help you find out about it. It doesn't help you establish what is in the text.

Scan to understand text quickly

Scanning can help you focus your search more. You do this by quickly looking over the text, following up any clues given to you in the index or contents page, to look for the exact information you need. Scanning text will help you zoom in on the information you need.

Scanning is a focused and shorthand form of reading. It involves:

- Picking out key words in the text
- Using key words as landmarks in the text so that you stay focused
- Saving time by not reading every word on the page in the hope of finding what you want

Scanning helps you spot the key words that are relevant to what you want to find out, so that you can then concentrate on reading the appropriate sections.

Reading texts, numbers and images can provide you with information that will help all aspects of your learning. You must make sure that you collect and record information that is relevant and in a form that will be useful to you later. Once you have located the information you need you should read it carefully making sure you understand what is being said. Skimming and scanning are not substitutes for reading properly, they are just techniques to help you find what you need to begin reading quickly.

When you come to make notes on something you will need to have read it properly making sure you either thoroughly understand what is written down or know what you need to get help in order to understand it. When you start reading a text properly you may have to go back to the beginning or a chapter of section in order to get a better idea of what the information is about. Once you have a clear understanding of the something you can start recording it.

Recording

You also need to record the relevant information you find so that you can:

- Return to it at a later stage
- Give the source of your information when quoting or referring to it in connection with your own work
- Compare it with other people's impressions

Making notes

Making notes is an important part of collecting information. Your notes provide a useful record of the information you have read and will help you to understand the text. When you come to write a report or essay based on your notes they will help you plan your work, be useful in helping you decide what to write and will also jog your memory. The ability to take clear notes will also help you revise for tests or exams.

You need to think carefully about the information you record as notes. When taking notes you need to ask yourself. 'Do I need this information?' and 'How and where will I use it?' Good notes are not simply passages of text copied out again in your own handwriting – you should try to use your own words. This will help show you understand what you are taking notes about and will mean that you are more likely to understand the notes when you read them later.

Leave spaces between notes and always have a margin. This gives you the opportunity to go back afterwards and add to them.

HINTS ON RECORDING INFORMATION

- Organise your notes around key themes written as headings
- Make notes on each text you read, with the author and title stated at the top and where appropriate the chapter or page numbers your notes come from.
- Note down real names exactly
- Always write down any quotations you intend to use exactly as they appear in the text your are reading
- Record exactly where the quote comes from because you will need to show this when you use it.

Once you have collected the information you need and recorded your findings you will be ready to summarise your material.

Summarising information

When summarising a text of some sort, for example, the content of a report or long article, your aim is to draw out the main points so that you can present it more briefly. You can do this by following these steps:

- Read the whole document through
- Read it again and highlight important bits
- Make a list of items to go in your summary
- Scan the document with your list in mind
- If you missed something, add it to your list
- Draft your summary and edit it
- Check your final draft and make any final changes necessary, then print it out

Writing documents

Effective writing at this level is about using the correct words and expressions in a way that communicates meaning clearly to everyone who reads it.

To make sure that you write what you mean so that others can understand it you should:

- Use a form that suits your information
- Organise your information so that it is clear and consistent
- Make sure your grammar, punctuation and spelling are correct
- Use images to help describe, explain or clarify ideas or information found in your written work and to break up the amount of text on a page

There is a range of document types that can be used for straightforward subjects. These include:

- Straightforward writing such as letters, memos, instructions, handouts, annotated drawings or diagrams
- Extended writing such as essays, reports, brochures or material to be used in the formal presentation of information to others

Types of document

Whatever type of written document you produce, you should:

- Check it for accuracy of content
- Check it for accuracy of spelling, grammar and punctuation
- Check it for appropriate tone
- Check if for clarity of meaning

Formal letters

Formal letters are used for business purposes. They are the main form of written communication sent to those outside the organisation, be it school, college, small business or large organisation. When used by an organisation, a particular 'house style' is usually followed by its employees.

There are three main formats currently used:

- Indented
- Semi-blocked
- Fully-blocked

The fully blocked letter is increasingly the preferred format. The following example shows the blocked letter format.

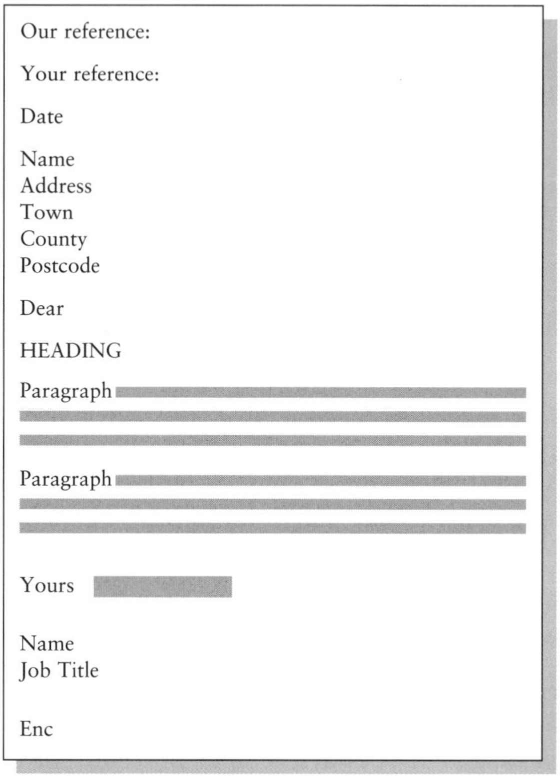

Our reference:

Your reference:

Date

Name
Address
Town
County
Postcode

Dear

HEADING

Paragraph ▨▨▨▨▨▨▨▨▨▨▨▨▨▨▨▨
▨▨▨▨▨▨▨▨▨▨▨▨▨▨▨▨▨
▨▨▨▨▨▨▨▨▨▨▨▨▨▨▨▨▨

Paragraph ▨▨▨▨▨▨▨▨▨▨▨▨▨▨▨▨
▨▨▨▨▨▨▨▨▨▨▨▨▨▨▨▨▨
▨▨▨▨▨▨▨▨▨▨▨▨▨▨▨▨▨

Yours ▨▨▨▨▨▨▨

Name
Job Title

Enc

Example of a blocked letter

Referencing a letter

The reference at the top of a business letter is often the initials of the person that wrote it and may include other numbers or letters to identify the department within the company that sent it, and even the reason for sending it. Here is an example:

EH/JS/44/CS99

Let's see how it breaks down:

- Eileen Hill (EH) is the person who wrote the letter
- John Smith (JS) is the person who typed the letter
- Cost centre 44 is the budget that paid for the letter
- Certificate Studies 99 (CS99) is the reason for writing the letter

When the company puts the letter into its filing system it will probably use this reference, so if you write a reply it is a good idea to quote it at the start. Perhaps you also have a filing system and give your letters references. Here is how you distinguish between the two:

Your ref: EH/JS/44/CS99
Our ref: whatever it is

You can substitute your own reference number for 'whatever it is'.

Open punctuation

Formal letters increasingly use 'open' punctuation, particularly in the blocked letter format, which speeds up the process of letter writing. Open punctuation means that some of the punctuation is absent. This does not mean that these letters contain no punctuation at all however, only that the use of simple punctuation is restricted to the body of the letter and removed completely from the reference, address, salutation and closing phrases.

UK date convention
day month year
4 December 2000

Starting a letter

Begin with the salutation 'Dear' followed by the title of the person you are writing to and then their name. Here are some common titles:

Mr	Master	Sir	Dr	Professor
Mrs	Miss	Ms	Rev	

The titles Miss and Master are generally used for children and young teenagers. Dr is the abbreviation for doctor; Rev is the abbreviation for reverend. Professor seldom gets abbreviated. With Ms and Mrs use whatever the individual prefers (don't work it out from their marital status).

Some people like to be addressed using a particular title and some people dispense with them altogether. Whoever you are writing to, it is a matter of courtesy to get their title correct. Use whatever title they have given in a previous letter; or if you have no previous letter, choose the title least likely to give offence. 'Dear Sir/Madam' is quite a safe way to begin.

Ending a letter

Two endings are in common usage:

- **Yours faithfully:** use it with Dear Sir or Dear Madam.
- **Yours sincerely:** use it for a named person, e.g. Dear Mr Smith.

For people you know fairly well, even in business, it may be appropriate to end with 'Best wishes' or 'Kind regards'.

Addressing a letter

Try to include these items in the address. Each one usually goes on a separate line

- Recipient's name
- Recipient's job title
- Recipient's department
- Name of the organisation
- Building name or number
- Street name
- Town or city
- Postcode

Recipient: the person who will receive your letter.

Heading a letter

Business letters usually have a heading after the salutation and before the main body of text. The heading tells the recipient what the letter is about. To make it stand out, you could put it in capitals or bold type, or perhaps underline it. One of them is usually enough.

Producing the body of a letter

Divide your letter into paragraphs that follow a logical structure. Use the first paragraph to mention any previous letters and the last paragraph to bring your letter to a close. Remember to be clear when explaining the purpose of your letter.

Key skill evidence

You can submit a formal letter as part of your key skill evidence. Either write a reply to a letter you have received or write to someone and invite them to write back. Here are some possible subjects for a letter:

- A planned activity or event
- A technical enquiry or issue
- Ideas or views
- A technical report
- Some statistical data

Use the flow chart below and remember that all letters have a purpose. Here are three ways to make your purpose clear:

- Include all the relevant information
- Use short sentences and simple words
- Fit your letter into one side of A4 paper

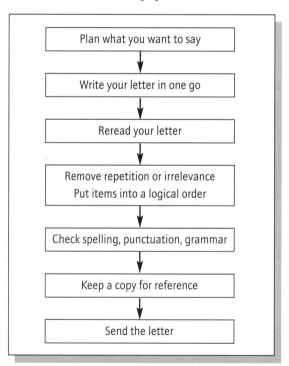

Memos

Memorandums, or memos, are sent between people within an organisation. They are rarely sent to people outside; letters are used for that. Memos should be short and straight to the point. Their purpose is to give or record information, and their format is designed to save time and space for both writer and reader. Memos are often delivered on paper but many are now sent by email.

You can submit a memo as part of your key skill evidence. You could write a memo drawing attention to:

- Several different ideas or several pieces of information
- A report containing technical information and/or data
- A series of activities or events

Memo headings

To	(who it's to)
From	(who it's from)
Date	(when it's written)
Subject	(what it's about)

MEMORANDUM

To

From

Date

Subject

Paragraph ▬▬▬▬▬▬▬▬▬▬▬▬▬▬
▬▬▬▬▬▬▬▬▬▬▬▬▬▬▬▬
▬▬▬▬▬▬▬▬▬▬▬▬▬▬▬▬

Paragraph ▬▬▬▬▬▬▬▬▬▬▬▬▬▬
▬▬▬▬▬▬▬▬▬▬▬▬▬▬▬▬

Typical memo format

Notes of discussions

People meet in groups to have all kinds of discussions, formal and informal. Sometimes you may need to record what happened, so note taking is a useful skill. If the notes are for your own use, they can be in any format you like but choose something you will understand when you come to reread them. Numbered headings and sub-headings may help you to organise them. You could use headings for major topics and sub-headings for minor topics. Here are some things to record:

- The main points people raised
- Decisions agreed by the group
- Important technical details and statistics
- Names of relevant people, places and objects
- Deadlines agreed by the group

- Agreed actions and who will take them
- Date of next meeting plus time and venue

Note taking is quicker if you abbreviate your words. Many words are still recognisable if you leave out their vowels (a, e, i, o, u). However you do it, use a system you can decipher after several days or weeks.

Promotional material

Here are some promotional items:

- Short leaflets
- Glossy brochures
- Posters in windows or noticeboards
- Billboard adverts

They aim to:

- Catch your eye with striking colours and images
- Keep your attention with interesting details
- Sell you a product by their overall persuasiveness

Promotional material needs to be interesting and attractive, clear and understandable. You must not break the law by:

- Making claims that are untrue
- Making claims you can't substantiate

Use language that readers will understand; trade jargon is normally unsuitable for a general audience. Try to get people on your side then they might buy whatever you're promoting. Avoid boring text and too much detail; they tend to turn people off. Incredible claims are sometimes qualified in small print; this could provoke criticism even when it is within the law.

Written report

A report is a useful way of presenting information and results from your projects or assignments. Here are some examples:

- A review of a product, performance or idea
- A progress record on a plan or proposal
- An outcome of an enquiry or investigation
- An account of an event, incident or happening
- A bulletin to highlight a technical problem
- A summary of a telephone conversation
- A digest of several other documents

Reports usually have this structure:

- **Introduction:** state your aims and purposes.
- **Middle:** present your findings.
- **Conclusion:** analyse and evaluate your findings.
- **Recommendations:** suggest what you think should happen next.

Some reports have extra sections:

- **For action:** concrete measures that come after recommendations.
- **Appendices:** important data, calculations, etc., put at the end.

The items in the appendices may be very important but they are often long or complicated and do not fit easily into the main body of the report. Putting them near the end makes them easy to refer to and stops the report's text becoming horribly broken up.

A more formal report may begin with its terms of reference – the people it's written for and the topics it's allowed to investigate – then a statement of its procedures – how it's allowed to gather information. Most reports are signed and dated at the end.

Use headings to guide readers through your report. Write a first draft then amend it, perhaps several times, to arrive at your final version. It should be easy to read and simple to understand. Before you submit your report, forget the words for a moment and see how it looks overall:

- Is your design good? Does it make an impact?
- Is it the right length? Not too much or too little?

BEFORE YOU WRITE A REPORT

- Check all the requirements, e.g.
  - word count
  - page layout
  - typefaces
- Check who you're writing for.

Prepare your first draft by jotting down the main headings followed by some brief notes. Indicate where you want illustrations, graphs or tables. When you come to write it:

- Keep an eye on the word count; don't write too much
- Assemble your ideas logically; don't jump about from one topic to another
- Don't repeat yourself

You may want to organise your text using numerical headings and sub-headings. This will help people to refer to particular parts of your report if they need to.

Essays

The essay form gives you an opportunity to use a range of writing styles. Listen to your tone of voice; you'll hear when it sounds right. The trick is to put the right words in the right places. If a sentence doesn't sound right, you can do two things:

- Keep the words the same but rearrange their order
- Keep the order the same but change one or two words

Here are some other guidelines to keep in mind:

- Hold the reader's interest
- Adopt a logical structure
- Always keep to the point
- Use clear, simple language
- Write short sentences

You can use an essay to:

- Present information you have gathered
- Compare two different viewpoints
- Discuss a range of different ideas
- Describe an event then comment on it
- Explore the nature of a problem

EVERY ESSAY SHOULD HAVE

- A beginning to say what it's about
- A middle to cover its main points
- An end to give appropriate conclusions

Communicating by email

Using email

Electronic mail, or email, is a system on the Internet which allows you to send messages and other computer files to any other user who has a computer connected to the Internet. When your computer is not connected to the Internet, the incoming messages are stored by your internet service provider (ISP).

The ISP has a computer which links you to the Web. You connect your computer to your ISP using a modem and a special phone number. Your computer will have an icon for dial-up connections. Click on this icon to dial into your ISP and check your email. You may need to enter a password. At work, college or school your computers may be permanently connected to the Internet.

An email program is computer software which lets you exchange messages with other users connected to the Internet. You can normally use it for these functions:

- Prepare and store messages before sending
- Send messages to other users
- Send messages to groups of users
- Receive messages from other users
- Scan and read the messages received
- Send a reply to any message
- Print out messages onto paper
- Send and receive computer files with messages
- Delete or store messages
- Store favourite email addresses

Email can be used to send and receive text, pictures, videos and sound. With some software packages it is even possible to make phone calls to another user who has similar equipment. All email programs work in the same general way and have the following basic features:

- **Header** is where you enter the email address of the person to get the message, anyone who is to get a copy, the subject of the message.
- **The body** is where you type the text of the message. You can cut and paste text from elsewhere, such as a word processor.

Online means connected to the Internet.
Offline means not connected to the Internet.

Email programs
Eudora
Outlook
cc:Mail
Hotmail/Webmail

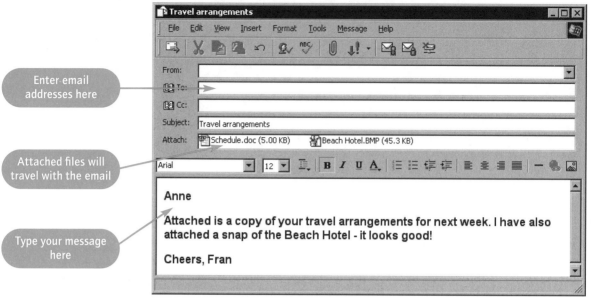

Enter email addresses here

Attached files will travel with the email

Type your message here

Creating an email with attachments

- **Address book** is where you can store the email addresses of people you know.
- **Signature** automatically adds your chosen signature and other details at the end of the message.
- **Reply options** let you return a message to the sender without typing in the email address.
- **Reply to all** lets you return your message to the sender plus anyone who was on the copy list.
- **Forward** lets you pass the email on to someone new, perhaps adding a comment of your own.

COMPOSE YOUR MESSAGES OFFLINE

If you are paying for your connection time, it is best to write your messages before you go online. You can then take your time and prepare several messages which are stored temporarily in your outbox. When you go online the email software can quickly send mail from your outbox and will get any mail which is waiting for you. New mail will appear in your inbox.

Sending email

- Select the command or icon for a new message.
- Use the **To** field to enter the email address you want to use. This address might be available from the address book icon at the top of the screen.
- Use the **cc** field if you are sending anyone a copy.
- Use the **Subject** field for your choice of short title.
- Use the body area to type your message. You can also use the paste command to import any clip art or other effects.

- To attach a file, use the appropriate command or icon then point to the place in your computer where the file is saved.
- When finished, use the **Send** command. If you are online the email will be sent. If you are offline the email will be sent next time you go online.

Receiving email

- Make sure you are online. For home computing this normally means selecting the icon of your internet service provider (ISP).
- The modem will dial your ISP and you may have to enter your password.
- Once you are online, use the appropriate command to download any messages from your mailbox held at the ISP.
- Any incoming mail is downloaded to your inbox; click on any new messages to open them.
- Read the message and perhaps reply by selecting **Reply**.
- Exit the message then transfer it from your inbox to a storage folder.

Email addresses

There are many millions of people on the Internet and there are many possible email addresses. You need to be careful when reading and writing an address you have been given. Although they may seem confusing, email addresses always follow the same pattern:

yourname@reallybigcompany.com

- **User name:** this is your personal address; it could also be two names separated by a dot, e.g. jim.jones, or an underscore, e.g. mary_jones.
- **Separator:** found on your keyboard, sometimes called the 'at' or 'axon' symbol.
- **Domain name:** an organisation has to register their particular name.
- **Type of domain:** helps to indicate the type of organisation, such as business, government, network and educational.

Netiquette

Etiquette means good manners, netiquette means good manners on the net. If you are emailing a stranger it is wiser to be polite, just as you would with a letter or phone call. Some suggestions:

- Don't shout with capital letters.
- Always fill the **Subject** field with a helpful title.
- When replying, don't return the whole of a message.
- Check the address before you hit **Send** or **Reply**.
- Wait and think before you reply.

Types of domain

.com	commercial
.org	non-commercial
.gov	government
.edu	educational
.net	network
.co.uk	UK commercial

Messages can cause embarrassment if they reach the wrong people or fail to arrive with the right people. You cannot recall emails once they are sent.

Emoticons

:-)	happy
:-(	sad
;-)	wink
:-0	shock

COMMON ABBREVIATIONS

AFAIK	as far as I know
BBL	be back later
BTY	by the way
FAQ	frequently asked questions
IMHO	in my humble opinion
RTFM	read the flipping manual
TTFN	ta ta for now

Grammar, punctuation and spelling

Grammar

Learning some basic rules of grammar will help to improve your communication. If you don't learn them, it probably won't stop you communicating but it may make your communication less effective. Understanding some basic rules of grammar may also increase your confidence in drafting your documents and presentations. Perhaps the best place to begin is with the parts of speech; have a look at the following table.

Part of speech	Explanation	Examples
Common noun	The generic name of a person, place, thing or idea	woman, city, pen, success
Abstract noun	The name for a feeling, idea, or opinion	joy, progress, prejudice
Proper noun	The title or name of something, someone or somewhere	the *Independent* newspaper the boy William the city of London
Collective noun	The name for a group of things	the *crew* of a ship a *flock* of sheep a *board* of directors
Personal pronoun	A word used instead of a noun; it avoids repeating the noun	I, he, she, it we, you, they
Adjective	A word that qualifies or describes a noun	some *beautiful* flowers John's *cuddly* toy a *difficult* idea
Conjunction	A word that links simple sentences or parts of a sentence	however, therefore, so but, and, yet, although
Preposition	A word that shows the spatial position of a noun	on, off, under, over beside, near, at, by in, to, from, through
Interjection	A short word that indicates an exclamation or greeting	oh, ah (exclamation) hello, goodbye (greeting)

continued overleaf

Part of speech	Explanation	Examples
Verb	A word that describes an action or thought; verbs drive sentences	I *send* you a message she *sends* him a memo
Tenses	The three main tenses are past, present and future	I sent a letter (past) I send a letter (present) I will send a letter (future)
Adverb	A word that qualifies or describes a verb	I think *quickly* She talks *quietly* They listened *impatiently*

Tenses

Muddles over tenses can lead to misunderstandings. Reread what you have written and check the tenses are okay. Do not jump confusingly between the past, present and future. If you're talking about the present, stay in the present tense; if you're talking about the past, stay in the past tense. Have a look at this extract about a meeting. Has the meeting happened or hasn't it?

> The manager **failed** to deliver the report on time because several of her support staff **are** ill. No one **is** available to help her meet the required deadline. However, she **is** able to provide a short oral update and **promises** to produce the report for the next meeting.

It's hard to say, isn't it? Things become much clearer when the extract is rewritten using the past tense throughout:

> The manager **failed** to deliver the report on time because several of her support staff **were** ill. No one **was** available to help her meet the required deadline. However, she **was** able to provide a short oral update and **promised** to produce the report for the next meeting.

So tenses add the dimension of time to your sentences to indicate that something has happened (past tense), is happening (present tense) or will happen (future tense). This is why you must be consistent when you use a particular tense.

Subject–verb agreements

Subject–verb agreement is about matching the subject and verb so they agree. It is a common source of problems. Singular subjects take 's' verbs and plural subjects take 'no s' verbs. Here are two examples:

The driver delivers.
The drivers deliver.

The woman walks.
The women walk.

As with all rules, there are exceptions. The exceptions are called irregular verbs. An important irregular verb is 'to be':

Present tense		Past tense	
Singular	*Plural*	*Singular*	*Plural*
I am	You are	He/she/it is	We are
You are	They are	I was	You were
He/she/it was	We were	You were	They were

Punctuation

Punctuation is about knowing how to start, how to pause and how to stop when writing in sentences. The punctuation marks are like signposts to the reader, helping them through your text without getting lost. Use punctuation to make your meaning clear or to achieve a special effect. If you are using a lot of punctuation, take some of it out. If your writing still makes sense then the punctuation was probably unnecessary. If your writing no longer makes sense or is ambiguous, try rewriting your sentences in a different way. Here are the punctuation marks you need to recognise and know how to use:

Punctuation mark	Symbol	Function
Full stop	.	To end a sentence
Exclamation mark	!	To indicate surprise or emphasise a point
Question mark	?	To indicate a question
Comma	,	To indicate a pause To separate items in a list
Semicolon	;	To separate sentence parts of equal weight To separate two contrasting points that appear next to each other
Colon	:	To introduce a list To introduce a long quotation
Inverted commas (quotation marks)	' ' " "	To enclose speech or quotations
Dash	–	To indicate a sudden break or to add a bit of explanation
Hyphen	-	To separate the parts of a compound word, e.g. short-term

continued overleaf

GRAMMAR, PUNCTUATION AND SPELLING | **47**

Punctuation mark	Symbol	Function
Apostrophe	'	To indicate ownership (the girl's book) To indicate omission (it's, don't)
Parentheses (brackets)	( )	To enclose an aside, something the reader can skip if they wish
Other parenthetical devices	– dashes – , commas ,	Use paired dashes or commas when you don't want the reader to skip
Ellipsis (three dots)	. . .	To indicate that part of a quotation has been left out
Square brackets	[ ]	Use square brackets if you insert any words into a quotation

Spelling

Some people think that poor spelling means poor content or lazy checking. This may not always be true but don't give people the chance to rubbish your good ideas just because you haven't spelt them correctly. Here is how you can improve your spelling:

- Learn the rules of spelling and their exceptions
- Read a variety of text and make a note of new words
- Always use a dictionary if you're unsure of a spelling
- Use a spellchecker when you're working on-screen

Have a look at these common spelling rules. Make sure you know all of them.

Ee sounds

i before *e*	receive
except	perceive
after *c*	deceive
e before *i*	weird
	seize

Prefixes (always at the front of the word)

add *in*	justice	injustice
	visible	invisible
	numerate	innumerate
add *il*	legible	illegible
	literate	illiterate
	legal	illegal

continued overleaf

Prefixes continued (always at the front of the word)

add *un*	safe	unsafe
	healthy	unhealthy
add *ir*	responsible	irresponsible
	regular	irregular

Suffixes (always at the end of a word)

add *ing*	agree	agreeing
	be	being
	go	going
drop *e* and add *ing*	confuse	confusing
	enthuse	enthusing
double the last letter and add *ing*	drop	dropping
	travel	travelling
	rebel	rebelling

Plurals

add *s*	book	books
add *es*	box	boxes
	fox	foxes
replace *y* with *ies*	company	companies
	industry	industries
replace *us* with *i*	radius	radii
	cactus	cacti
replace *f* with *ves*	thief	thieves
	loaf	loaves
no rule, so memorise	woman	women
	man	men
	person	people
	child	children

Watch out for words that sound the same or similar but have different spellings. Here are a few common examples:

beach by the sea, *beech* as in tree
cereal for breakfast, *serial* on TV
council in the town, *counsel* with advice
dear in my heart, *deer* in the forest
draft on paper, *draught* in the air
find after searching, *fined* for breaking the law
forward in motion, *foreword* in a book
principal mainly, *principle* idea

seen by a witness, *scene* of a crime
sauce for food, *source* of information
earn for a living, *urn* like a vase
wait while attending, *weight* that you lose

Part 2: The Bottom Line

This part concentrates on what you must do to get your key skills qualification. It will show you:

- The words and ideas of the key skills.
- The difference between level 1 and level 2.
- How you can practise the skills.
- What must be in your portfolio of evidence.

This part is divided into four sections:

- **What the unit expects:** This section will explain the evidence requirements of the communication key skill, and how to put your portfolio together. Your portfolio is the key to getting your key skill – this part of the book tells you how to choose your evidence and get it ready.
- **Evidence for level 1**
- **Evidence for level 2**
- **Other forms of assessment and evidence:** This section will tell you about the external assessment and how to prepare for it.

Qualifications and Curriculum Authority
The key skills specifications are published by the QCA, and are widely available through schools, colleges, training establishments and awarding bodies. They are also available on the QCA website (www.qca.org.uk).

What the unit expects

What does straightforward mean?

Communicating about straightforward subjects is a key feature of levels 1 and 2. The word 'straightforward' is used to identify the standard expected of you. The good news is that most of your work or interests could be called straightforward; avoid getting involved in something more complicated than you need to.

Straightforward
simple
uncomplicated
clear-cut
not confusing
routine
elementary

What's the difference between level 1 and level 2?

You need to be clear about the level of key skill you are collecting evidence for. This may depend on the GNVQ you are taking. For a Foundation GNVQ the appropriate choice is level 1 communication. For an intermediate GNVQ the appropriate choice is level 2 communication. For GCSE remember that roughly speaking, level 1 is the same as a GCSE at grades D to F, and level 2 is the same as a GCSE at grades A to C. Try to achieve a key skill at the highest level you can. However, it is always a good idea to make sure you at least achieve the key skill appropriate to the other qualifications you are taking.

What is level 1 all about?

At level 1 you will see there are basically three types of evidence that you need to provide. The key skill unit at level 1 asks you to show that you can apply your communication skills and provide evidence for the following three areas:

- Discussions (one-to-one and group)
- Reading for information
- Writing documents

You can collect the evidence for each of the three areas from different places if you like. For example, one GNVQ unit, one GCSE or one other qualification might be great for showing that you can write documents but it might not be the best opportunity to show you can discuss something. A better opportunity might exist in another part of the qualification you are doing. At level 1 especially, you should use your best opportunities to collect evidence where you can.

How is level 2 different?

You will need to provide different types of evidence for communication at level 2, the intermediate level. Level 2 is a harder level to achieve and it will involve showing you can:

- Work at a harder level
- Give a short presentation
- Take part in a group discussion
- Read and summarise larger documents
- Produce a longer piece of writing

The first point to note is that some of the evidence requirements are different. You need to show that you can work with more difficult sources of information, you need to have a wider range of oral communication abilities (you need to give a short talk as well as take part in a discussion), and you need to show you can produce more demanding written work.

> ### ORAL COMMUNICATION
>
> Oral communication is communicating through speech or talking. The key skill requirements involve judging your ability to speak to other people and with other people. You will be assessed to see if you have the skills needed to take part in discussions and can give short talks about certain topics.

What about your portfolio?

Building your portfolio of evidence

Your portfolio of evidence is the work you have done to prove to your teacher and others that you can do what the key skill asks you to do.

> ### EVIDENCE
>
> Evidence is the proof that you can do what is required in order to get the key skill. It is proof that you have learned about communication and that you can use and apply what you have learned.

The simplest approach to collecting and keeping your evidence is to have a separate folder or portfolio for your communication evidence. This is by far the easiest way to organise your work and keep a record of what you have done and what there is still to do. Consider the following ways to organise and label your work:

- Have a contents page that you keep updating as you build up your evidence.

- Keep records of when you collected your evidence and where it came from (e.g. which GCSE or GNVQ unit).
- Get into the habit of writing down the purpose of your work as you collect evidence.
- Use the key skill sections to divide up your portfolio. At level 1 they are called 'discussions', 'reading and obtaining information' and 'writing documents'.
- Copies of work are acceptable if the actual key skill evidence is part of another course; the original work can be kept with the course that it comes from,
- Keep a checklist of all the things you must cover in your portfolio (e.g. in the presenting section you must show you can use one chart and one diagram).

A key skill unit is quite a large amount of work. It is the same size as a GNVQ unit and just a little smaller than a GCSE. So you may have to carry out several different tasks to have sufficient evidence to show you can meet the key skill requirements.

Evidence for level 1

Taking part in discussions

Background information

This part of the key skill is asking you to show that you can be an active participant in discussions. The key skill is trying to see whether you can contribute (say something) in discussions and participate in other ways as well. This means contributing, listening, encouraging others, helping to involve others.

What kind of group?

You don't need to be part of a big group, a small discussion group will do. Ideally, you want enough people interested in the topic to make it a good discussion. The important thing is to have people who are interested in what will be discussed. You also need to be interested. This will make the investigation into the topic more enjoyable. You are also likely to learn more from those who are interested in the topic. Get involved with people you are comfortable discussing things with. This will help you to feel less nervous about saying anything. It also makes it easier to encourage others to take part if you know them well.

Choosing a discussion topic

You should consider using the discussion as an opportunity to help you understand a part of another course you are taking. You could discuss the topic, ask others questions and use it as an opportunity to clear up things that you may not understand or are not sure about. This gives you a chance to find out what others think. You might be able to use the discussion as an opportunity to get ideas; for example you could discuss how to tackle a design problem or how to investigate a subject that you need to do for another course. Try to decide on a topic that you will be able to benefit from in other ways rather than just providing evidence for your communications key skill. This could be a topic in your GCSE course or a GNVQ unit. The different courses or units you do will give you lots of opportunities to discuss different things. Choose something that really interests you or will be useful to discuss. Even if you choose to discuss something not related to any course you are doing, perhaps, a hobby or interest, make sure you do it with others who are also interested. This will

mean that you can learn something from them. You will need to have at least two different subjects to discuss. You need one subject for your group discussion and the other for your one-to-one.

What about the one-to-one discussion?

Make sure you have something to discuss that gives you an opportunity to show you have all the necessary skills. A couple of quick questions and a few yes/no answers won't do it. You might be sharing an opinion you have with a teacher, classmate, friend or customer (if you are using work or work simulation to generate your evidence). You might be looking to clear something up that you don't understand. The topic itself doesn't really matter. You still have to do some work to prepare for the discussion, show you can make relevant contributions, show you can listen and show you can meet the other requirements.

What you must learn to do?

Investigate the subject

You are expected to do a little work before the discussion, finding out about what is to be discussed. This will help you develop a point of view on the subject based on what you have been able to learn. You will have developed an informed opinion and as a result should have some valuable contributions to make in the discussion. This is all about doing some preparation before you discuss the topic.

> ## INFORMED OPINION
>
> When you know about a subject because you have read up on it and have taken the time to learn something about it, you are said to have an informed opinion. Your opinion is informed by the investigating you have done.

Know when to contribute

Here are a few simple rules about politeness:

- Never interrupt someone else
- Never cut across someone
- Never talk over someone

Being impolite and forcing your contribution into the discussion means you are making inappropriate contributions. Show you can wait for the right moment. Learn how to make the right contribution at the right time. Make sure what you say is appropriate and fits in with what is being discussed. Try not to change the subject or say something just for the sake of it. These are both signs of not knowing when to contribute something.

Making relevant and appropriate contributions

- **Relevant contributions:** this simply means making the right contribution at the right time. Don't introduce things that have nothing to do with the discussion or were to do with something that has already been discussed. If something might sound like it is not going to be relevant, take time to explain to the group why you think it is. This is to help them understand. If you have prepared questions and points to make and the opportunity to use them doesn't come up or they no longer seem right, make a note saying why you didn't use them. This is evidence to show you can tell whether something is relevant or not.
- **Appropriate contributions:** this refers to making appropriate comments. For example, if the discussion is a brainstorming session then suggest ideas and help come up with solutions, don't sit back and offer nothing or, worse still, criticise the contributions others make.

Speak appropriately

This part refers to using an appropriate tone of voice, manner, behaviour

> ## BRAINSTORMING
>
> When you get together with others to try to come up with ideas about something. You share your ideas and add to the ideas of others.

and type of language. Using inappropriate language, tones of voice or behaviour are all signs that you cannot make suitable contributions. Speak clearly and make yourself understood by the rest of the group.

Pay attention

Even when you are not talking, you still need to be working to earn this part of the key skill. You need to show that you are an active listener, paying attention to what others say and showing that you are open and interested in their points of view. There are several ways you can do this but the most obvious is to ask questions related to what they said. Remember that you can use non-verbal communication to show you are paying attention.

Collecting evidence

All examples are designed to get you to start thinking about what you need to do. You will be able to add in more information based on your own circumstances.

HOW TO OBTAIN YOUR EVIDENCE

What you need to do	Holding a team meeting	Holding a one-to-one
Group discussion Show you can contribute to a group discussion about a straightforward subject in an effective and positive way. You need to show you can contribute information relevant to the discussion and that you can speak clearly in a suitable way. You also need to show you can listen to others in the group properly and respond to them in an appropriate way. **One-to-one** Show you can take part in a one-to-one discussion about a straightforward subject in an effective way. You need to show you can contribute information relevant to the discussion and that you can speak clearly and in a suitable way. You also need to show you can listen to the other person closely and respond in an appropriate way.	You could be working with others on a project of some sort. It could be anything from making something to carrying out some market research or doing a survey. You will be able to generate evidence by having regular, organised team meetings, perhaps with a chairperson, someone taking minutes or notes and an agenda. Having an organised meeting will mean having to conduct yourself in an appropriate manner. Create opportunities to discuss work by having items of the agenda that you all need to talk about and that the Chairperson needs to have some agreement on or an answer to. This should help you show you can contribute and help play a part in reaching an agreement or making a decision. This doesn't have to be a one-off event. You might find that over time you become more confident and can make more effective contributions and play a more effective role in these meetings.	Meeting with a teacher or classmate to discuss a topic that you don't fully understand. This should give you plenty of opportunities to explain your problems, listen to answers and to ask follow-up questions. Your purpose is clear and there is something you definitely need to get out of the discussion. In practical subjects you might have to design and make something. This will mean lots of opportunities to discuss work with the teacher or a work partner. Having a discussion with a customer or manager in a workplace situation, as part of a job or work placement. Make sure there is some record of the discussion that could count as evidence to show you met the requirements. This might be a letter from the other person involved in the discussion or a witness testimony.

Evidence requirements in a nutshell

You are going to have to do two types of discussion: one in a group and the other in a one-to-one situation. You need to discuss different things each time you can't talk to the person in the one-to-one about the same things you discussed with the group. You need to discuss something that is straightforward; it doesn't have to be complicated.

Whether one-to-one or in a group, you need to demonstrate these four things:

- Say things that are relevant
- Say things clearly and in a suitable way
- Pay attention to other people
- Respond appropriately to what they say

HINTS FOR DISCUSSION

- Write down a brief paragraph about your discussions. Include things like who was in the group, why these people were group members, what topic was discussed, the time and the date. You could also include how long you discussed things for.
- Try not to dominate the group by speaking all the time.
- When you prepare for the discussion, note down any points you want to discuss and any questions you wish to raise. Keep these notes as evidence for your portfolio.
- Make a few notes about how well you think you did in the discussions. Use short headings and look at how you did in each area.

Reading and obtaining information

Background information

This section is a lot easier to do if you have a clear purpose for finding out the information. You could be doing an investigation into a topic that you will discuss with others. Perhaps this could be for your communication evidence for discussions. You might be doing some research for an essay or report that you have to write. You might be using your written work as evidence of writing documents. You might be doing course work for a GNVQ or a GCSE, or you might be writing a letter. Whatever it is, it will be a lot easier if you have a clear purpose – a reason for reading and obtaining information.

What you must learn to do

Get advice and help from other people

You need to show that you know when to ask others for advice or help, particularly when you are not sure about something you have read and you need to check it out. You might be trying to obtain instructions on how to do something, you might be trying to find out the best place to get information or you might be trying to discover what people think. The type of information isn't that important; you just need to know how to ask for advice.

Work out the main points

Get hold of what you need to read then show that you can read it, identify the main points and make sense of them. You can read books, newspapers, magazines, websites, CD-ROMs, letters, brochures or leaflets. You need to show that you can read and understand information about straightforward subjects. This means the material doesn't have to be complicated, lengthy or difficult.

One of the documents you read will need to contain at least one image and you need to show you can understand the information it contains. The image can be a picture, sketch or drawing; a chart, diagram or graph. It could even be a map. Newspapers often have images and text to read and understand; this would be ideal.

Use a dictionary

Dictionaries can help you understand words that might be confusing.

Getting information ready to use

Get the information you need and assemble it for your purpose. You might write up the information as notes to use in a discussion, or you may want to use the information in a report or essay you have to write. It might even be a letter or a memo that you need to write and the information you gather will be useful in helping you write it. The key thing is having a reason or purpose for reading and obtaining information. When you have the information you need, prepare it so you can use it. If you are going to use the information in your notes for a discussion, highlight the parts that will be very important to discuss. This will help to draw your attention to them or remind you about them.

Collecting evidence

What you need to do	Preparing for a discussion	Other examples
Show you can get hold of information from two different types of document. One of the source documents has to have an image that you can understand and use. When reading both these documents you must show you can: • Find out what information is relevant to you • Understand the main information that is relevant to you • Use this information effectively for your purposes	**Purpose** Collecting information about a topic to be discussed as part of your course. **Topic** Could be anything relevant to the course you are taking. **Types of document** Consider looking up the topic on a CD-ROM encyclopedia like Encarta (or a regular encyclopedia). There might be images involved here. There could be magazines, newspapers or books that have relevant information. You could also consider searching the Internet. You could write up what you found out as: • A series of brief notes that contain the points you want to make or share with the group in the discussion • A list of questions you want to ask • A list of points or issues you want the group to discuss	• Prepare notes for an essay or report, then use them for evidence on writing documents. • Look up manuals or guides to find out how to do something by computer. A lot of computer manuals use images. • Decide which is the best or most suitable deal when buying something. There are lots of different magazines that you could use to help you decide. • Look at a newspaper and see how it covers a news story. The editorial section is a good place to find opinions. • Look at the letters page in a newspaper and identify the opinions there.

Evidence requirements in a nutshell

Read two different types of document to get information you can use later on (this is your purpose). You might use this information in a discussion, an essay or report, a letter, a memo or anything else that has a clear purpose. One of the documents must have an image and you must show you can understand it. For each document:

• Find and understand the information you need
• Sort out what's relevant and what isn't
• Prepare what you've learned in a form you can use

Writing documents

Background information

This aspect of the key skill requires you to produce two different types of documents about straightforward subjects. One of the documents must contain at least one image.

What you must learn to do

Produce different types of documents

This part of the key skill is about being versatile, showing that you know how to produce written documents properly. The documents can be business letters or memos, reports or essays, webpages or email. They should contain important information; you can't use short notes to friends. You need to become confident in producing a range of written documents. You will probably have to produce written work for your GNVQs, GCSEs or your job, so use this as an opportunity to brush up your skills. Use course work to provide evidence for this part of the key skill.

Using images

You are also expected to use images to communicate information to people reading your work. These images can be charts, graphs, diagrams, sketches or drawings. The aim is to see that you can use images effectively to support the points you are making in your written work. Images can help readers to understand your points more easily.

Select what is relevant

When you've collected all the information you need, show how you judge the best information to use. Decide what is most relevant and how much information will do:

- **What is most relevant?** You will probably find that some of the information you have collected will be better at supporting the points you want to make than others. You must show that you can decide what is the best information to use, then use it effectively to make your points. Don't put in information that won't help support your points just because you've collected it. This will only increase the amount of writing you'll need to do without adding anything important and it'll take the attention of the reader away from what you really want to say.

- **How much will do?** This is what is meant by sufficient. There is no point in using every little piece of information you collect, because you could be repeating yourself. You must show you can judge how much information is needed to make your points and then use this information effectively. This way your work will be to the point and it won't bore people who read it.

Spell words correctly

Show you can do the basics of written communication correctly to make sure that your text is understood. Check your spelling, make sure your sentences are formed correctly and make sure your text is organised correctly.

Collecting evidence

HOW TO GET YOUR EVIDENCE

What you need to do	Document without an image	Document with an image
You need to write two kinds of document.	A letter asking for some information to help you with a project you are doing.	Advertising material like a brochure or leaflet about a local event you're involved with.
Each document must be about a different subject. In one of these documents you must use an image to help you make your point.	Make sure you explain exactly what your project will be about and the type of information or help you need.	The image could be a picture (perhaps using clip art on your computer) or it might be a map to show how to get to the event.
The information contained in both documents must be relevant, written and presented in an appropriate way.	Make sure the letter is properly laid out. Check your letter yourself and ask others to read it to see if they understand.	Written information would have to be written clearly and laid out in an interesting way to catch people's attention.
It must be clear and easy to read; the spelling, grammar and punctuation must be correct.		If you are creating a leaflet make sure you do enough work to meet the evidence requirements.

Evidence requirements in a nutshell

You must produce two types of document – that's the most important point. In one of these documents you must show that you can use an image of some sort (your choice) to help you make your point. Make sure the image is clear, it has a title and it relates to the point you're trying to make.

The information that you use in the documents must be relevant. People must be able to read the text and understand what you mean. Make sure your punctuation, grammar and spelling are correct.

HINTS ON WRITING DOCUMENTS

- Create a plan for your work and put it in your portfolio. It can show early thoughts on organisation and the development work that you have done.
- Keep any drafts that you have made, especially the drafts that show your edits and any changes to punctuation or grammar. Don't be afraid to reveal your mistakes in early drafts because this shows you can spot them and correct them yourself.
- Print out a clean copy of your final written work to keep as a record of your finished document. This may sound obvious but you might be submitting a clean copy of your work as evidence for another course.
- A computer can help you with spelling and grammar. Microsoft Word and other word processing packages have spellcheckers that automatically show your mistakes as you make them.
- Keep backup copies of your work when you use computers.

Evidence for level 2

Taking part in discussions

Background information

This section of the key skill is asking you to show you can take part in discussions. The key skill is trying to see whether you can contribute in discussions and be an active participant. This means contributing, listening and keeping the discussion moving forward.

What you must learn to do?

Contribute effectively

- **Vocabulary and expressions:** you need to show you can change the words and phrases you use to suit the different types of contributions you want to make. The key skill is looking to see if you have developed skills to make you a flexible contributor in discussions; for example, you should be able to present an argument, share you ideas and opinions and exchange information depending on the type of contribution needed at the time. Your contributions need to be clear and relevant to the discussion. Check you have made yourself understood. For example, if your contribution involves a complicated argument or point that needs to be made, you should use appropriate techniques to help get the point across and make sure others understand it.

- **Adapting to circumstances:** before making any contribution, think about the nature and composition of the group and the topic under discussion. This is because it is not enough to make clear and relevant contributions. You also need to show you can suit the circumstances. Your contribution should be appropriate for the group and the topic. For example, it may be a formal gathering, or an informal group; you must keep this in mind and adapt your contributions and behaviour accordingly. Your tone of voice is important and so is your manner. Make sure both are suitable and appropriate for the topic being discussed and the group you are discussing it with. The topic under discussion may be sensitive and your contributions should be suitably phrased. If it is a serious topic then being flippant or insincere is

failing to make a contribution that suits the nature of the topic and may be offending those in the group who intend to treat it seriously.

- **Coping with controversy:** if you think your contribution is controversial, then you need to present it sensitively. If it is too controversial then you probably need to show a little self-discipline and self-censorship. Try not to react if your argument or opinion is not accepted by others or is not treated properly by others. This is someone else showing they are not able to participate effectively. Respond politely and let it go.

Listen and respond

- **Listening to others:** even when you are not talking, you still need to be working to earn this part of the key skill. You need to show that you are an active listener, paying attention to what others say and showing you are receptive to their contributions. There are several ways you can do this but the most obvious is to ask questions. When you ask questions, take account of what other people have said. Your body language can also show you are paying attention. A good way to show these skills is by being attentive.

Attentive: being alert and paying attention.

- **Responding appropriately:** there are several ways of responding appropriately. Politeness is always appropriate. Other ways include answering questions or points made by making sure you address the issues properly and don't ignore them or answer a different question (the one you hoped the person would ask). You can ask follow-up questions, politely ask for clarification if you don't understand something or refer to what others have said in your contributions. All are ways of responding appropriately. An important skill that you need to develop is the ability to be tactful.

Tactful: to deal with people or situations by showing consideration, sensitivity and awareness of other people's feelings.

Recognise people's intentions

This is really about showing that you can interpret the signs that show what others are feeling when they make contributions. This means understanding how to interpret people's manner, tone of voice and vocabulary. There will also be a chance to show you can interpret and understand non-verbal communication.

Develop points and ideas

You could be developing points through questioning, perhaps by asking someone to develop an idea they contributed or by asking them to explain something further. You could develop a point yourself. When the discussion wanders off the point, you could help to bring it back by summarising what you think the relevant parts were and then highlighting what still needs to be discussed. You are showing how your contributions help to keep the discussion moving forward and help to explore the different viewpoints that exist.

Collecting evidence

What you need to do	Brainstorming	Team meetings
Take part in a discussion about a straightforward subject, showing you can make contributions that are clear, relevant and suit the occasion. During the discussion show that you can listen to others and respond to them in appropriate ways. Show that you can keep the discussion moving in the right direction.	Your group has to come up with ideas about how to do something. It could be a project to design something or to do some other group work (e.g. a survey). Make sure people know what is going to be discussed. This will allow them to prepare and come up with ideas. Agree that you need a result at the end of the discussion. This could be an agreement, a decision or an answer. This need to get a result will help you and others keep the discussion focused and moving forward.	When you use team meetings as opportunities to generate group discussion evidence, concentrate on the agenda items where decisions need to be taken. Make sure there is plenty of time for a full discussion. Keep records of the meeting (agenda, notes, etc.) and make sure someone is taking full minutes of the meeting. You can use the minutes as evidence in your portfolio. Make your own notes about the seating arrangements, who's who, key decision points, who said what, and keep notes on points you wanted to make.

Evidence requirements in a nutshell

You need to take part in a discussion, making contributions that suit your purpose and are appropriate given the situation and circumstances of the discussion. The subject under discussion doesn't need to be complicated.

- Keep your own contributions clear and relevant.
- Listen and respond to what others are saying in an appropriate manner.
- Play your part in moving the discussion forward.

HINTS ON DISCUSSION

- Write a brief paragraph about the context of the discussion. Include things like the make-up of the group, the topic under discussion, the time and the date.
- Try not to dominate the group with your contributions.
- Prepare for the discussion by doing some research into the topic and making notes on the points you want to discuss or questions you might like the group to address.

The Bottom Line

Giving a short talk

Background information

Part 1 considered some ways to make your short presentation as accessible as possible. You don't have to demonstrate all these techniques. You just need to show you can identify some key factors that will be important to your audience and then show you can take account of them when you make your presentation.

Practice is important; it is the key to presenting. You are not expected to develop presentation skills overnight or meet the requirements at the first attempt. Take time to develop the necessary skills. Practise and rehearse on your own or with friends. The more presentations you do, the better you will become. This is how you gain confidence and experience. So practise and try out different techniques in different situations. Try to look for opportunities to develop your skill by making small-scale presentations in a range of circumstances. Even if you practise by doing just one or two minutes, this will help you gain confidence. Practise techniques like eye-contact, voice quality and how you stand.

Start simply with brief presentations about straightforward topics, then build up your skills from there. This will also allow you to practise using visual aids like OHTs.

What you must learn to do

Prepare and structure your presentation properly

- **Preparation:** make sure your presentation is suitable for the occasion and adapted to fit your purpose. A presentation about a design concept might involve some sort of graphics and strong visual images. A contribution in a debate will need to address other people's arguments and use powerful and persuasive language. Think carefully about sharing any results, so the information is communicated in a clear and interesting way. Know your subject well and do whatever research you need to. You'll have your talk notes to prepare, you might have an OHT to create and you'll have an appropriate image to select.
- **Structure:** your presentation will also have to be arranged appropriately. This means organising your presentation to allow others to follow it easily, helping them to recognise the key messages and to understand your information. Help others follow your line of thought by mentioning when you are introducing new points, by making it clear when you are coming to an end and by making your conclusions conclusive.

Match your language to subject and audience

Try to avoid slang and avoid words that are needlessly complicated or showy. Stick to clear, plain English. Use technical language only when it's relevant and always explain it clearly to the audience

Always check your understanding of difficult vocabulary and consider using a thesaurus to identify alternatives that may be simpler and help more people to understand. A thesaurus is also useful to help you create alternative ways to explain complex points or ideas.

Thesaurus: a book containing lists of words with the same or similar meanings.

This is the time to practise your techniques to hold the group's interest and attention during your short talk. Remember to vary your tone of voice, use gestures and non-verbal communication techniques to keep the group's attention. There are other techniques you can use when you write your notes, e.g. devising examples to suit your group.

Using images

When you have a difficult point to make or an important issue to raise, use an image to help you. Most data is more interesting as a graph than as a table; it may even be more memorable.

You are really trying to show that you can select an image to help others understand an important part of your talk. You are trying to show how you explain something using more than words alone. This means you need to spend time selecting an appropriate image that really does help you explain something well or will help others understand your point more clearly.

Collecting evidence

HOW TO GET YOUR EVIDENCE

What you need to do	Sharing some results	Presenting a design
Give a talk about a straightforward subject. Make sure you use an image to help you explain your main points during your talk. Show you can speak clearly and in a suitable way, sticking to the subject. Organise your talk in a way that helps others follow what you are saying.	When you have done some project work that involves experiments, surveys, questionnaires or some other sort of investigation, you can present you findings or results. The main advantage of doing this form of short talk is that you know your topic best. This will help to give you confidence. You could use an OHT to show a table of results, a graph or pie chart to help the group understand your results.	If you are doing a practical subject (e.g. Engineering, Design and Technology), you could present your final design ideas to the group. The structure of the presentation could take the audience through how you met each of the design requirements. Your image could be a drawing, diagram or model of the product. You are talking about your ideas and this should give you confidence.

Evidence requirements in a nutshell

You must give a short presentation to people about a straightforward subject. During your presentation you need to show that you can use an image

of some sort to help the audience understand what you are saying. There are three important skills to demonstrate during your presentation. The first is to speak clearly and appropriately. The second is not to waffle or wander. And the third is to organise what you say so people can follow it.

HINTS ON GIVING SHORT TALKS

- Take time to prepare your notes; you can use them as part of your evidence.
- Keep a copy of the image you use; note how, why and where you used it.
- Write down details like the time, length, topic of your presentation and what you knew about the group you were talking to. Explain how you organised things to make your presentation more effective; this helps others to understand why you developed it as you did.
- Practise with friends or family and don't be afraid to ask for advice or constructive criticism.

Reading and summarising information

Background information

Extended documents

textbooks
other non-fiction
company reports
newspapers
magazines
journals
webpages
essays

You need to produce a straightforward extended document. A straightforward document should use a simple structure to present easy information. You don't have to use difficult sources of information or complicated sources of information.

Extended documents are long documents. You must not use brief documents or short documents. Articles should be more than three pages long. This is to give you a chance to demonstrate that you can skim or scan documents to find the information you need.

A document may be almost anything you read. It needn't be a book or a magazine; it could be taken from a website, a collection of images or a program listing.

What you must learn to do

Find relevant information using different sources

This can be any type of information. For example, you might be doing a little research into a topic for another course, you might just be looking for instructions for something or trying to find out some useful facts and figures.

Identify the information you need

This key skill requirement focuses on your ability to skim sources of information to find the material you need. This means you need to have a clear idea about what you are looking for and how to recognise it when you see it. You are not expected to read through every word on every page. This is why the key skill talks about scanning and skimming. You are expected to locate what you need to know in a quick and efficient way.

Detect a writer's intentions

This is about interpreting what you think the writer's thought were by looking at the words, tone and structure the writer uses. Each can help form an impression of the writer's intentions. This is really asking you to see how others use tone, vocabulary and structure to suit their purpose or their intended audience. This is something you need to consider in all aspects of your work. It is important in discussions and presentations as well as in writing documents. Here you have an opportunity to see how others do it.

Recognise the key message in text and images

Show that you can find and understand the key message or point the writer is trying to get across. The requirement to use at least one image is another attempt to develop skills that make you versatile and able to interpret text and images. There are words or phrases that should tip you off about a writer's key points or conclusions. Look for words that can be used as a way of signalling main points or thoughts, such as: therefore, so, however.

Summarise the information

Develop an informed opinion about a topic and present it somehow. You could be writing it up in a report or essay, presenting it to a group or turning it into notes to help inform a discussion.

WHAT YOU MUST LEARN TO DO

- Use two appropriate information sources.
- Quickly zoom in on the information you need.
- Read and use sources of reference to help you understand.
- Spot any bias and compare different sources.
- Draw together and use information from different sources.

Collecting evidence

HOW TO GET YOUR EVIDENCE

What you need to do	Choosing a product	Researching an essay
Identify and read information about a straightforward subject using two extended documents.	The two extended documents are from a specialist magazine that reviews your chosen product and an appropriate book. There are several magazines that advise you on the best computers, games consoles, cars, etc.	The two extended documents are two different explanations of the same historical event or person. For example, different opinions about why or how something happened or how important different factors were. You can compare explanations and make up your own mind.
One of the documents must have at least one relevant image.		
Produce a summary of the information taken from both documents that shows you have correctly identified the main points and messages the writers wanted to get across.	Try focusing on two different reviews of the same two products: two competing cars, computers, or whatever. This way you will get the different writers highlighting different features, making different points and perhaps even disagreeing. You could then look at the reviews and make up your own mind.	You can gather other information to help you understand key concepts from encyclopedias, CD-ROMs and the Internet. The end result will be an accurate account of each explanation. You will also try to use these sources to help form your own opinion.

Evidence requirements in a nutshell

You need to find out about a straightforward subject, showing you can read and understand, then summarise information from two extended documents. Make sure one of the extended documents has at least one image; you need to show you can read and summarise information from the image too. You must show you can:

- Choose and read relevant material in the extended documents you use.
- Identify and understand the main points of text and images.
- Summarise the information and adapt it to your purpose.

HINTS ON READING AND SUMMARISING INFORMATION

- Note down why you are doing the reading and summarising.
- Keep notes on each of your sources; include the authors, publication details, and maybe quote a few passages.
- Keep copies of anything that might be useful as evidence (e.g. keep a copy of the image you use).
- Note down your own opinions on what you read and explain how you arrived at them.

Writing documents

Background information

This aspect of the key skill requires you to produce two different types of documents about complex subjects. One of the documents you produce must be an extended document including at least one image. The key skill gives you an idea about how long an extended document should be. It mentions essays or reports of more than three pages.

What your must learn to do

Select an appropriate style and form

You need to show that you can make decisions about how to present your work effectively. Part of this is choosing a style that suits the nature of the subject and the type of document you are writing. This means using persuasive techniques when you are presenting an argument, or knowing how to present evidence, facts or information to support your work. Presenting facts and figures may be your opportunity to use diagrams or charts in your text. You may also use technical language if it is appropriate.

See also: **Using jargon**, page 2.

Vocabulary, style and tone can all be adapted to suit your reader and your purpose. Compare how the tabloids (*Sun*, *Star*, *Daily Mirror* etc) and the broadsheets (*Guardian*, *Times*, etc.) present the same news story. Newspapers adapt the news to suit their readers and sell more copies.

Take relevant information and present it clearly

You are being asked to show you can organise your written material appropriately. This means making effective use of paragraphs, headings and sub-headings. You are not trying to show off complicated words and technical language. You are trying to communicate a straightforward subject in a clear piece of writing.

Write clear sentences with accurate spelling

Do the basics to make your text understandable. You need to form your sentences correctly and put punctuation marks in the right places.

HOW TO GET YOUR EVIDENCE

What you need to do	*Extended essay or report*	*Other documents*
You need to show that you can write two different types of document about straightforward subjects. One has to be an extended document including at least one image. Your documents must show you can select and use an appropriate style of writing and organise your text to suit your purpose. Your meaning must be clear and your text must be legible. Spelling, grammar and punctuation must also be accurate.	Normally you need to write up the results of any fieldwork or surveys you do. This gives you a great opportunity to produce an extended document including an image. Your results can be used to generate a graph, chart or diagram, and then incorporate it into your text. This will help you get key information across to the reader. This type of document also allows you to develop a structure for your work that helps lead the reader through the text. Introduce what you did and explain why you did it. Explain how and when you went about your investigations, then explain what you found out. Draw any appropriate conclusions. Make sure the headings and sub-headings clearly highlight this structure. You can use your results to support your conclusions. These points will help you meet the style and structure requirements.	**Letters** There will be particular styles, structures and conventions depending on the type of letter you intend to write. Make sure you use an appropriate style. If you are using a computer, look at the letter templates that could be available in the word processing package you use. Make sure the letter will be long enough or about topics that will let you show what you have learned about written communication. This way the letter will be a better form of evidence. **Memos** Memos can have different forms and styles and they can be used for different purposes. This will provide an opportunity to show you can use effective styles and structures. There are memo templates on many word processing packages. Review your work early on to ensure it will generate the evidence you need for your portfolio. **Other possibilities** Brochures, leaflets or newsletters provide opportunities to use images, structures and styles.

Evidence requirements in a nutshell

You are going to have to write two different kinds of document (perhaps a report and a letter). One of the documents has to be an extended document, which means it has to be more than three pages and it must contain at least one image (e.g. a chart, a graph or a diagram). Each document must show you can:

● Present your information, using an appropriate structure and style
● Write legibly with correct spelling, grammar and punctuation

---

HINTS ON WRITING DOCUMENTS

● Create a plan for your work and put it in your portfolio. It can show early thoughts on the development work you have done.

● Keep the different drafts you have made, especially the drafts that show your edits and any changes to punctuation or grammar. Don't be afraid to reveal your mistakes in early drafts because the this shows you can spot them and correct them yourself.

● Print out a clean copy of your final written work to keep as a record of your finished document. This may sound a little obvious but you might be submitting a clean copy of your work as evidence for another course.

● Keep backup copies of your work when you use computers.

Other forms of assessment and evidence

External assessment at levels 1 and 2

You will need to take an external assessment as well as produce a portfolio of communication evidence. The external assessment is designed to show that you can do communication tasks at the correct level under a different set of circumstances. You might be asked to do the assessment in a single long session or in several shorter sessions. This is up to your school, college or assessor to organise for you.

What is the point of an external assessment?

The idea of an external assessment is that someone else sets you a series of communication tasks, then gives you all the information you need to get on with them. That way you can show that you can carry out different communication work to complete tasks set by other people. Your portfolio shows that you can use communication to carry out your own tasks.

It is also attempting to show that you can do larger, related tasks under controlled conditions, such as a time limit, and with someone else setting the tasks. Here is how to look at the portfolio and the external assessments:

- The portfolio shows that you can set your own communication tasks to meet your own deadlines and time constraints.
- The external assessments show that you can carry out larger, related communication tasks set by other people and meeting the imposed time limits.

When you meet these requirements, you will get your key skill in Communication, you will have proved that you can do the communication work under a range of different conditions and in different contexts.

Part 3: Opportunities

This part highlights opportunities for generating communication evidence in the qualifications you are taking. It will show you:

- How your qualifications can be used to generate communication evidence.
- Where the best opportunities for this evidence arise in the qualifications.

This part is divided into two sections:

- **Evidence from GCSE courses:** You will find this section useful whichever awarding body you are with.
- **Evidence from GNVQ courses:** This section will be useful at both foundation and intermediate level, regardless of whether you are working towards a full award or a Part One award.

The examples provided should be seen as starting points for generating evidence. You will see that some qualifications provide more opportunities than others. However, all contain some opportunities and will at least get you started. Make sure that you take time to read not just your subjects but also subjects that are related to the ones you are taking. This will help you gain a fuller understanding of how and where number evidence can be produced. For example, if you are doing a Business GNVQ then look also at the Business Studies GCSE and the Retail and Distributive Services GNVQ. You may also want to check out the Leisure and Tourism GNVQ.

At level 1 you do not need to give a short talk or presentation, and the documents you read, summarize or write do not need to be lengthy. However you should always attempt to develop and use your skills at the highest possible level.

Vocational awards
The GNVQ Advanced awards are now called Vocational A-levels. From September 2001 GNVQ Foundation and Intermediate awards are likely to be known as Vocational GCSEs.

Evidence from GCSE courses

Art GCSE

About the syllabus

The Art award helps you to develop your creative, imaginative and practical skills as you work in art, craft and design. You will also have the opportunity to explore historical and contemporary sources and make practical and critical judgements and responses.

See also: **Art and Design GNVQ**, page 110.

Topic area 1
Images and artefacts

Discussion

The progress you make in art, craft and design will be judged by the development in the work you produce. Images and artefacts will be produced as the result of exploring and developing ideas and carrying out investigations into art, craft and design. Investigations into art, craft and design can take a variety of forms. You can discuss:

- Ideas with your tutor
- Working as part of a team
- A piece of work with its creator
- Advice from a librarian or gallery assistant

You will also be expected to be able to use your images as a source for discussion. It is as important in art, craft and design to know what you have done as it is to decide what you want to do. You can discuss your work:

- In a one-to-one with your tutor
- During a short presentation or talk to others
- When evaluating your finished work

Some artists, craftspeople or designers do not like to discuss their work. They say that the work speaks for itself. As you develop your art, craft and design skills, you should be prepared to discuss your ideas and your completed work with others. At level 2 you can give a short talk, which will help you to explore:

- Different ways to present ideas
- When and how to use technical language

- How and what others think about art, craft and design
- How to adapt your talk to your audience and your purpose

Reading for information

Another way to explore and investigate art, craft and design is through using different written sources. These sources can be used to:

- Give you ideas
- Provide technical information
- Follow up items that interest you
- Build up your subject knowledge

You will need to record what you find out. All artists, craftspeople or designers keep records of some kind but they are described in different ways:

- Sketchbooks
- Notebooks
- Visual diaries or logs

The important thing is that you find ways of recording or summarising the information that is important to you. This could be through sketches, notes, tables, charts, colour swatches, scrapbooks. Remember, for these records to be meaningful, you must organise them so you can use them again. Some artists may not use ideas for several years but they know where to find their records when needed.

Writing documents

Many people do not associate artists, craftspeople or designers with writing. They think of them as doers and makers. For some artists, crafts-people, or designers writing is an important part of their creative process. Writing is used for:

- Discussing work such as in an exhibition catalogue
- Recording ideas and evaluating work such as in a visual log or sketchbook
- Reviewing the work of others in a magazine or brochure
- Exploring and investigating creative ideas with others as in letters between artists, craftspeople, or designers

Your programme will expect you to:

- Investigate the work of other artists, craftspeople and designers
- Evaluate your own and others people's work

When you explore and evaluate art, craft, and design you will have the opportunity to produce an essay on the work of someone you admire or are interested in. You will need to:

- Organise your ideas
- Structure the essay to make your meaning clear
- Use sketches, drawings or images to support your thinking

Opportunities

- Use relevant technical language
- Write it clearly and present it well

Topic area 2
Personal project

Discussion

All art schools expect you to undertake a personal project as part of the course. The programme expects you to develop skills for working across all aspects of art, craft and design and you will have the opportunity to produce work from direct experience, observation or imagination using any medium, material or technology available. Choose a subject that is meaningful to you. Discuss the starting point with your tutor. It does not always have to be visual. Discuss where you will find out more information. Artists use a range of different sources:

- Music and sounds
- Novels and poetry
- Ideas and overheard conversations
- Images and objects

Remember, the more you discuss your work with others, the more likely you are to find out the strengths and weaknesses of what you are doing. This will help you to become more confident and creative.

Reading for information

Texts of all types are a rich source of stimulation. You should learn how to skim and scan texts to select what is important to you and what is not, what is relevant to your project and what is not. Always record your findings in notes, sketches, lists or charts so that you can use them later.

Writing documents

Written information comes in many different forms. You will already have produced some as you made records from discussions or reading and research. Make sure you understand the purposes of your writing. You may have written:

- A letter asking for information on an artist, craftsperson or designer
- Notes to support your work
- Annotated drawings or sketches to remind you of colours, textures or time of day
- An essay on an artist, craftsperson or designer
- A technical report on developing a new making technique such as how to work with colours or use a dark room correctly and safely.

Always make the purpose of your writing clear and use established conventions. Handwritten work should be legible. Essays should be properly punctuated and include correct grammar and spelling, especially with regard to specialist vocabulary for art, craft and design.

Further opportunities for evidence

Other people's art, craft and design

You are expected to show an appreciation and understanding of the work of other artists, craftspeople and designers, and make connections between their work and yours. These investigations will lead you to look at a range of different secondary sources such as magazines and books, essays and catalogues, films and videos, webpages and complete websites. You should look carefully at how creative individuals use written and spoken language, both as a tool to explain their activities and as a means of extending their creativity.

Galleries and museums

You will have the opportunity to see examples of art, craft and design at a range of locations. Each venue will explain, promote or support the exhibit with a range of different forms of communication. They will have:

- Publications on the artist, craftsperson or designer
- Videos or interactive displays that explain the work on view
- Guided tours or lectures on the exhibits
- Audio guides and written gallery plans
- Labels and notes to explain the exhibits

Notice how the spoken and written language varies according to audience, context and purpose; use your observations to develop your own communication skills.

What you must know
Part 1: The Learning Curve will help you with the knowledge you need.

What you must do
Part 2: The Bottom Line will help you with the evidence you need.

Business Studies GCSE

About the syllabus

The Business Studies award helps you to develop your ability to apply your communication skills and demonstrate knowledge and critical understanding of how businesses work in a wide range of contexts. You will be required to select, organise, interpret and use information to help evaluate the strengths and limitations of ideas and distinguish between facts and opinions.

Topic area 1
The aims and objectives of business

Discussion

You will be expected to understand how an organisation works within a range of economic, political and social contexts. This understanding of a business will include the structure, the nature of the business, the aims and objectives and the criteria for judging success. To do this you will need to learn how to select, organise and interpret information from a range of sources. You will need to develop and use your skills of speaking and listening to collect information through:

See also: **Business GNVQ**, page 114.

- Discussions with your tutors
- Discussions with others following the same course
- Interviews with people who work in your chosen business

Once you have developed an understanding of how a business runs, you should take the opportunity to check this out with others. You could do this through:

- A one-to-one with your tutor
- A short presentation or talk for others
- Feedback to the business you studied

You may be concerned that you do not have sufficient confidence to give the short talk or presentation required at level 2. However, you need to develop the ability to speak to other people, discuss things with them and present information for them; it should not matter whether you know them well or hardly at all. This will help you to explore:

- Different ways of presenting business concepts, theories and practice
- When and how to use technical language and terms
- How to respond to questions from others on your ideas, judgements and conclusions
- How to adapt what you say according to the audience and the purpose of your presentation

Reading for information

Another way to collect information on business practices is by using different written or text-based sources. These can be a source of:

- Factual information
- Technical reports and bulletins
- Opinions in magazines or newspaper.

You will need to be able to skim through extended documents such as reports, research papers and textbooks to identify the information you need. Make sure you can tell the difference between facts, opinions and ideas. Learn to recognise differences of intention by the vocabulary, tone or structure of the text. Identify the main ideas and summarise them in a notebook. Remember that you are reading and summarising information for a purpose. You must be able to find information easily within your notes.

Not all information is presented in text. Important information is often presented using diagrams, charts, tables and graphs. It is important that you can read and understand this information particularly when it refers to income, market share and profitability.

Writing documents

You will have the opportunity to produce an essay or report on your analysis of businesses and their functions, their success or failure. You should use technical terms alongside business concepts and theories to explain how the business you have chosen works.

You will be expected to support your conclusions using charts, tables and diagrams that show growth, profit margins or projected increase in market share. Make sure the structure of your report or essay makes your findings clear. Where you give an opinion or make a judgement, make sure it is supported by evidence.

Write in short, clear sentences. Do not obscure your meaning in difficult words or awkward phrases. Proof-read your work to check its grammar, punctuation and spelling.

An extended piece of writing is not the only way to present findings. You may wish to create a set of overhead transparencies to combine your written and oral skills. If you take this approach, remember to strike the correct balance between what you say and what you put on the transparency.

Topic area 2
Human resources

Discussion

The way a business structures itself, its roles, relationships and management are important aspects of your programme. You will be expected to understand and explain the role of the human resources and personnel department in:

- Recruitment of new staff
- Motivation of the workforce
- Training of staff
- Intra-organisational communication

You may find out more about each of these topics through meetings and interviews with the human resources or personnel managers from different companies and compare them with the approaches to recruitment and staff development in small or medium enterprises (SMEs). If you have the opportunity to discuss human resources with a manager or employer, remember to adapt what you say and how you say it to your particular context or setting. Take along a set of questions and perhaps tape the discussion so you have a record of it.

Try to be aware of the other person's intentions by taking notice of their manner, tone of voice or body language. Use your time effectively; keep the discussion moving forward. Make sure you understand what they are saying; if you are unclear about something, ask them to repeat it or to explain it in another way. You could also check your understanding of what they are saying by repeating it to them in your own words.

At level 2 an interview or a piece of personal research can be used to form the basis of a presentation or a short talk to your tutors or others on the programme. Remember, they were not part of the interview, so you will need to:

- Prepare your talk properly
- Adapt it for your listeners

- Create a structure for your talk (you could use your original questions as the main headings for your talk)
- Use images to help convey your points (for example, a chart of the management structure)

Reading for information

Businesses produce a range of documents; here are some of them:

- Mission statement
- Business plan
- Management structure chart
- Job descriptions
- Personal specifications
- Job advertisements

Each document has a particular function and is written in a particular style. Some businesses or companies have a house style – a style they follow in all their documents. House style can include:

- Typeface and point size, e.g. 10pt Times Roman
- Use of capitals and punctuation
- Specified formats for correspondence

By looking at a company's documents you can tell a lot about how it treats its staff – how it recruits them, how it trains them, how it promotes them and whether it values them. Here are some of the things you could identify:

- The importance of certain jobs by the advertisements used to recruit for them
- Attitudes to staff by the nature and form of information made available to them
- Opportunities for staff development by the range of training programmes made available
- The management structure and its hierarchy by the management chart and the line management structure

You will also have the opportunity to explore both internal and external business or company conventions. These may include:

- House style or preset formats for memos or letters
- Time taken to reply to customers
- Time schedules for issuing contracts or delivery of goods and services

Summarise your findings so you can use them in any final presentation, evaluation or report.

Writing documents

An evaluation of a company's human resource management provides you with an opportunity to present written information supported by images. Structure your material to make your judgements and conclusions clear and use the correct conventions for written work, e.g. grammar, punctuation and spelling.

You may wish to produce:

- A summary of business communications containing different styles such as those used for memos, letters, job descriptions, personal specifications and job advertisements.
- A set of overhead transparencies which summarise your main findings for use in a presentation.
- An extended report in which images such as diagrams and drawings show management structures and job functions.

Whichever form of written communication you use, try to balance your presentation so the impact of your work is supported by the clear use of appropriate techniques.

Opportunities from production and marketing
All businesses have a product and all products must have a market if the business is to survive. An analysis of how individual businesses work out how to identify a market, communicate with the market and promote products within the market, will provide you with a wealth of information on how communication techniques and marketing objectives are combined by successful businesses.

What you must know
Part 1: The Learning Curve will help you with the knowledge you need.

What you must do
Part 2: The Bottom Line will help you with the evidence you need.

Design and Technology GCSE

About the syllabus
The Design and Technology award helps you to develop your knowledge and understanding of designing so that you can work with appropriate and suitable design specifications to communicate your ideas. You will be expected to develop your making skills by applying knowledge and understanding of relevant processes, materials and techniques and by using materials, tools and equipment.

Topic area 1
Working with a design specification

A design specification can be presented orally, supported by diagrams or drawings, or in the form of a written text supported by other relevant data. You will be expected to develop an understanding of the design specification through discussion with your tutors and others following the same programme.

Discussion will help you to explore and develop:

- Different types of vocabulary and expressions as you analyse the requirements of the specification
- Your listening skills as you are briefed on the materials, technologies and equipment needed
- Your ability to respond appropriately as you clarify or confirm your understanding

See also: **Engineering GNVQ**, page 119; **Manufacturing GNVQ**, page 136.

Opportunities

At level 2 you will also have the opportunity to present your interpretation of the specification to others. You will need to use appropriate presentation techniques and language to present ideas on form, function and possible making processes.

Reading for information

You will also need to explore and interpret a range of sources to obtain relevant information on media, materials and equipment. These sources could include:

- The design specification itself
- Manufacturers' technical guides for materials
- Safety manuals for items of equipment

You may need to make notes to act as an aide-memoire to be used later. You should not copy out large sections of these manuals but skim through them to:

- Find the relevant section
- Identify the important points
- Produce a summary for later

You can record items in a sketchbook or notebook. You may also choose to annotate the diagrams or drawings included as part of the design specification.

Writing documents

Writing documents of any length may not be associated with design and technology. All the communication skills are very important in this subject. Writing is as important as the other aspects. It is used to:

- Make notes to help you realise your design
- Record your investigations as you work on the specification
- Annotate diagrams or schedules to help you realise your design
- Evaluate your own work or other people's work

Design solutions are usually supported by an oral presentation but you may wish to prepare overhead transparencies (OHTs) or a PowerPoint presentation to support this evaluation and presentation. Effective OHTs will be clearly written and effectively organised to ensure other people can follow what you have done and understand the main points.

The clarity of your presentation and the technical accuracy of your language skills may determine whether or not you can inspire the person who gave you the original design specification and persuade them you have a good design solution. Make sure that you proof-read and re-draft your work if necessary. Grammar, punctuation and spelling do matter; they are an essential part of presentation.

Discussion

Before you begin making anything, you must fully understand the original specification. Check your understanding by discussing the specification with your tutor. Prepare properly for this discussion and be sure you know:

- What questions to ask
- When to seek clarification
- When to ask for something to be repeated
- How to end the discussion satisfactorily.

You may not have the opportunity to return to ask questions again later so make sure you can summarise the main points.

Talking to others about your ideas will help you to identify the strengths and weaknesses in your plans; it will also help to clarify matters, confirm ideas or test your design thinking. Oral presentation at level 2 usually takes place:

- When you have prepared your design ideas in the form of diagrams, drawings, maquettes or models
- When you have completed a prototype or produced a final object or artefact

Always be clear about the intention of your talk and decide when during the process you will deliver it. Remember that a talk or presentation is not an argument. You may be giving the talk but you must also listen and respond to others.

Reading for information

Once the preparation is over and you have begun to make something, you will probably use these sorts of reading:

- Checking with your design ideas
- Reviewing the making schedule
- Referring to notes on techniques or use of equipment
- Consulting annotations on your plans or drawings

The accurate and careful interpretation of these sources will make an important contribution to your final outcome. Make sure you understand any instructions or notes before proceeding. Always record any changes to plans or procedures so you can include them in future developments or evaluations.

Writing documents

Working drawings, annotated diagrams and a production schedule should support your evaluation of your final outcome. This information could be presented as an extended technical document with suitable headings and sub-headings to help readers follow your evidence. Wherever possible, use

Opportunities

the precise technical language associated with the making process, especially when describing media, materials and technology.

The extent to which your work in design and technology provides evidence of your communication skills will depend upon the quality of your writing, particularly your style, your clarity and how they are supported by your grammar, punctuation and spelling.

Further opportunities for evidence

Class work activities

The learning programme you follow will provide you with the opportunity to practise your communication skills. You will have to separate tasks, which will require you to:

- Work collaboratively with others and discuss joint activities
- Find ways of obtaining and remembering information
- Researching information in textbooks, manuals and specifications
- Writing evaluation pieces on your work or other people's work
- Practising how to record ideas, information and findings
- Observing how others use communication techniques effectively

What you must know
Part 1: The Learning Curve will help you with the knowledge you need.

What you must do
Part 2: The Bottom Line will help you with the evidence you need.

Course work assignments

Your programme of study will require you to undertake a project in which you will be expected to combine communication skills, design skills and making skills. Designs may be communicated through drawing as well as through discussion and writing. Your project will provide you with an opportunity to find the most appropriate means of combining the different dimensions of communication to develop and present your ideas effectively and to analyse and evaluate your final products with clarity and accuracy.

English GCSE

About the syllabus

The English award helps you to demonstrate your ability to develop your communication skills including speaking and listening, reading and writing. You will be required to organise and adapt your speaking skills to suit different situations and audiences. You will be expected to read a range of English prose, poetry and drama and to be able to distinguish between fact and opinion, follow an argument and select information for a purpose. You will also learn how to write in a variety of forms or genres using accurate spelling, grammar and punctuation. In developing these abilities, you will use many of the communication key skills:

- Contributing to a discussion
- Giving a short talk or presentation
- Reading and summarising information
- Writing for a specific purpose

Topic area 1
Shakespeare

You will be expected to study at least one of Shakespeare's plays as part of your programme. Do not worry that these plays were written hundreds of years ago; they cover the same ideas and themes that you are familiar with in today's films, plays or videos. The main differences are Elizabethan:

- Elizabethan English
- Elizabethan settings
- Elizabethan attitudes

Discussion

To help you understand the context or setting of Shakespeare's plays you will have the opportunity to discuss Elizabethan England with others. Discussion will help you to explore and develop:

- Different types of vocabulary and expressions as you analyse Shakespeare's use of language and the technical terms to describe it such as blank verse, iambic pentameter.
- Listening skills as other people describe their understanding of Elizabethan England, the context or meaning of Shakespeare's language, the themes his plays address and the characters they portray.
- Your ability to respond appropriately as you clarify or confirm your understanding of what other people have said.

At level 2 you will also have the opportunity to give a short talk or presentation. You will need to prepare yourself properly by assembling notes on topics such as Shakespeare's contemporaries or the role of theatre in Shakespeare's England. Use the correct technical language in your notes.

Reading for information

Each of Shakespeare's plays has been written about, described and analysed many times, and different critics draw different conclusions. You will need to look at a range of them. The primary source is the play itself in its unabridged form. You will also have access to secondary sources that:

- Describe the themes within the play
- Outline the plot and sub-plots
- Explore the characterisation
- Provide a critical analysis of the play's structure
- Translate selected words, phrases and expressions

You will need to be able to skim through this material to identify the relevant sections, then scan them to identify the information you need.

Through your use of secondary sources, you should develop the ability to:

- Differentiate between fact and opinion
- Detect the writer's intention
- Identify the main line of reasoning
- Summarise key messages or points

Writing documents

Writing is important in English and communication. You will be expected to write essays on a range of topics. The focus will depend on your tutor's guidance but here are some possibilities:

- **Empathy**: when you imagine yourself to feel like the character in a scene; you must show understanding of the character's emotions and reactions.
- **Literary criticism**: when you will be expected to describe how characters behave and the relationships between them; how language and other effects create atmosphere.
- **Performance**: when you show an understanding of how the words on the page are transformed into actual performance; this is made easier if you have seen the play performed live or on television, film or video.

You should structure each piece of writing to help readers understand your meaning and follow your descriptions or arguments.

When describing events or explaining the use of language in the plays, use the technical expressions you have learned through your study of literary criticism. Make sure that your style of writing is fit for purpose. Empathy or writing in role will require you to use the first person and the present tense whereas literary criticism will use the third person and the past tense. For each type of writing, express your meaning clearly and use accurate grammar, punctuation and spelling.

Topic area 2
Imaginative or original ideas

Discussion

Class, group or paired discussions are often used to stimulate ideas and provide a starting point for you to explore and share thinking with other people on your programme. These informal discussions provide an ideal opportunity for you to practise your speaking and listening skills. You should always:

- Speak fluently and with confidence
- Use standard English (or Welsh)
- Practise new words and learn from other people
- Listen to what other people say
- Adapt your language to engage attention

At level 2 you will also be given the opportunity to present your ideas, finished piece of prose or narrative to other people. Make sure you adapt your language to suit the subject:

- Remember that standard English may not be appropriate
- Vary the tone of your voice to retain interest
- Change the pace or expression to signal changes in the narrative
- Use images or sound effects for impact or atmosphere

Reading for information

The imagination needs to be stimulated and the work of others provides a basis for ideas, storylines, characters, contexts and, most importantly, the use of language for dialogue and description.

Your programme will give you access to other literatures besides English. Use reading as a source of ideas and a means of improving your vocabulary. Note which types of literature and which writers capture your interest and try to see how they have succeeded. Effective creative writing includes:

- An engaging plot, theme or storyline
- Believable characters
- A noticeable or evocative atmosphere
- Imaginative or effective use of vocabulary
- A coherent structure
- Accurate grammar, punctuation and spelling

Take every opportunity to build up your experience by keeping notes of interesting characters and storylines, words and phrases you have noticed.

Writing documents

The first draft hardly ever flows; you seldom begin at the beginning and keep writing to the end, uninterrupted and without any changes. You will need to plan your writing and make decisions about:

- The type of prose, poetry or narrative you wish to use
- What the basic storyline will be (flow diagram)
- The characters, their main qualities and roles
- The connections between characters (spider diagram)
- The setting or context for the piece of writing

Your plan should also follow the simple structure of having a beginning, middle and end:

- The beginning should set the scene, introduce the characters and describe the setting. Indicate the plot without giving too much away.
- The middle should be built from your spider diagram by developing the characters. Your use of vocabulary and structure will help to develop the plot and help readers to follow the narrative
- If you have planned properly, the ending will not be a cliché. An ending should bring everything together in a resolution, leave the main issues open as in many modern stories, or introduce something unexpected yet plausible.

Each of these approaches will give you the opportunity to produce writing for a specific reason and to develop techniques for handling structure, lan-

guage and purpose. How much they can contribute to your communication key skill will depend on how you have been able to balance them with accurate use of language, including grammar, punctuation and spelling. Redraft your work until it reads well and proof-read it to check for mistakes.

Opportunities from technical writing

You will also be given opportunities to learn how to approach informative writing and persuasive writing. This will include:

- Memos
- Formal letters
- Leaflets
- Advertisements
- Reports

You will need to use your skills to communicate ideas or information, to express your own opinion and to persuade others to change theirs. The skills you use in producing these different kinds of writing and the evidence you produce should contribute to your evidence for the key skill of communication.

Geography GCSE

About the syllabus

The Geography award helps you to develop your knowledge and understanding of places, environments and patterns on a local scale and a global scale. You will be required to use your developing knowledge and understanding to show an appreciation of the environment and human interaction with it. You will do this by developing and applying a range of skills, many of which will develop and promote the skills used in communication. They include:

- Speaking accurately and knowledgeably about geographical matters
- Discussing and presenting geographical issues
- Reading and summarising geographical information accurately
- Presenting written geographical information supported by maps and diagrams

Topic area 1
Geographical enquiry

You will be expected to develop your geographical skills using primary and secondary sources. Primary sources include:

- Interviews and discussions with others
- Listening to others give talks or lectures
- Collecting evidence from site visits or fieldwork

What you must know
Part 1: The Learning Curve will help you with the knowledge you need.

What you must do
Part 2: The Bottom Line will help you with the evidence you need.

See also: **Leisure and Tourism GNVQ**, page 132.

Secondary sources will include:

- Other people's records
- Photographs, maps, diagrams
- Statistical data prepared by others

Discussion

You will be expected to discuss ideas with your tutor in a one-to-one tutorial or work with others on your programme during a group discussion. The focus of your discussion may include planning and preparation for a site visit. This will involve:

- Sharing ideas and opinions as you work out a schedule
- Exchanging information as you agree roles
- Listening closely and checking you have understood
- Summarising discussions about your site visit

At level 2 you will also be in a position to lead a discussion or make a presentation on the focus of an enquiry. Prepare properly and think through what you want to say. You will need to:

- Support what you say with photographs, maps or diagrams
- Make sure your audience understands what you say by using English (or Welsh) and explain technical terms
- Present your information clearly and logically to help listeners follow your line of thought or the events or ideas you are describing

Reading for information

Geographical enquiry will often involve work on a national, international or global scale. Communication skills must then be used to read, interpret and summarise these secondary sources. You will need to access a range of different sources to obtain relevant information. You will be expected to:

- Differentiate between facts, opinions and ideas
- Skim sources to locate appropriate texts
- Scan texts to identify valid information
- Identify analytical, descriptive and interpretative writing
- Record and summarise the main points from texts

Writing documents

As well as presenting your findings orally, you will be expected to communicate information and ideas in writing supported by images such as maps or diagrams. You will be expected to bring together your summaries to evaluate your findings and draw conclusions. This may take the form of an essay or report.

Always structure your written work to help readers follow your analysis, descriptions and interpretations. Wherever possible, use the technical language of geography to add precision to your text and to make your meaning clear. Use your communication skills to support your geography

skills by proof-reading and, where necessary, redrafting your text to improve the grammar, punctuation and spelling.

Choose different ways to present your information. A balance between different forms that suit the purpose will help you to present evidence in valid ways that support your evaluation.

Topic area 2
Economic matters

Discussion
Economic geography will usually be taught using secondary sources such as:

- Population figures and distributions: local, regional and national
- Trade figures, including export and import statistics and exchange rates
- Reports and research papers from governments and the EU
- Textbooks, videos and CD-ROMs

These sources will provide you with an opportunity to obtain information that is relevant to your enquiry and they will enable you to discuss your material with other people.

Other people may not interpret the information in the same way as you. They may not hold the same opinions or views, or they may have developed different ideas. These differences will allow you to develop your discussion and presentation skills as you debate the geographical issues before you.

Remember that a discussion is not an argument; always listen to what others have to say and respect their right to take their turn in discussion. Try to be aware of body language, tone of voice and vocabulary; yours and other people's. It may be appropriate to prepare your own notes before discussions take place, and also to make notes of other people's contributions.

Reading for information
Economic geography seeks to be as current as possible, so besides textbooks, you will be expected to research texts that are found in newspapers, magazines, research reports and the webpages of the government.

You will be expected to check the accuracy of facts and data by cross-referencing them with other published information. You may also need to question the accuracy or validity of evidence that you have read.

As in other aspects of geography, skimming and scanning are important skills in locating and collecting evidence. Make sure that key points or ideas can be substantiated by other sources such as charts, tables or diagrams.

Writing documents
Ideas and information in economic geography cannot be presented clearly using text alone. This will provide you with the opportunity to use draw-

ings or tables and charts to confirm your findings, support your conclusions or clarify your ideas.

Make sure that you structure your material to help your readers understand your report and follow your line of reasoning. This may involve cross-referencing or the inclusion of annexes. Use an appropriate style of writing and clearly identify your supporting evidence.

Any evaluation of your work should include a review of the skills you have used and the means by which your evidence was collected, presented and analysed. The extent to which you do this effectively may determine the level at which you are developing your communication skills.

What you must know
Part 1: The Learning Curve will help you with the knowledge you need.

What you must do
Part 2: The Bottom Line will help you with the evidence you need.

History GCSE

About the syllabus
The History award helps you to develop your understanding of how the past has been represented and interpreted and how you can use this understanding to examine historical sources critically. You will be required to use your developing knowledge and understanding of the past alongside skills of investigation, analysis, interpretation and evaluation to draw conclusions about periods, societies and situations. Your study of history will help you to develop and apply a range of skills that are relevant to the key skill of communication:

- Speaking accurately and knowledgeably about historical matters
- Discussing and presenting historical issues
- Reading and summarising information from historical sources accurately
- Supporting historical information with drawings, diagrams and maps

Topic area 1
Understanding of chronology

You will be expected to develop your historical skills using primary and secondary sources. Primary sources will include:

- Interviews and discussions with others
- Listening to others give talks or lectures
- Collecting evidence from site visits
- Analysis of original documents

Secondary sources will include:

- Other people's records of events
- Photographs, drawings, maps, diagrams
- Statistical data prepared by others

Discussion
This involves developing an understanding of:

Opportunities

- When events took place
- The order in which they happened
- The time between them

You will be expected to discuss ideas with your tutor in a one-to-one tutorial or work with other people on your programme during a group discussion.

Discussions with other people will help you to develop a clear understanding of chronology, context and sequence. Listening to what others have to say will help you judge the accuracy and validity of your own descriptions, explanations and understanding of events. Often you become more able to grasp who did what and when, as you listen to others people's interpretations and have the opportunity to comment or ask questions.

At level 2 you are required to give a short talk or presentation. Presenting your ideas on causes, consequences and changes will require you to structure what you say to help listeners follow your talk. The chronology of a series of events is one way of providing a framework to help you explain and for your audience to understand.

Chronological order or sequence can be effectively represented graphically:

- A time line can be used to show the sequence of events
- A tree diagram can be used to show the relationship between people and events
- A flow diagram can be used to show how one event led to another
- A map or plan can be used to show the interrelationship of armies, countries or cities

Reading for information

Historical enquiry often involves understanding the key features and characteristics of periods, societies or situations. You will be expected to read a range of primary and secondary sources to identify relevant information and then interpret and summarise it for your own purposes.

The communication skills you need to access a range of different sources include:

- Finding and identifying relevant sources of information
- Reading to differentiate between facts, opinions and ideas
- Skimming identified sources for appropriate text
- Scanning texts for relevant and valid evidence or information
- Identifying a writer's reasoning and apparent intentions
- Recording and summarising information for later use

To decide whether or not a piece of writing can be taken at face value, look at its context, its date and its setting:

- Documents written during wars are highly likely to be influenced by a political perspective.

- The economics and cultural attitudes of the time will influence evidence concerning trade in the nineteenth century.

Always look closely at the style of what you are reading and check whether the text is trying to:

- Analyse
- Describe
- Interpret
- Persuade.

In conjunction with the time it was written, this will tell you a great deal about its authenticity and validity.

Writing documents

As well as presenting your findings orally, you will be expected to communicate information and ideas in writing supported by images. You will be expected to bring together your summaries to evaluate your findings and draw conclusions. This may take a variety of forms including essays and reports. A clear appreciation of the chronological context will help you to describe and explain ideas, attitudes and beliefs held by people at the time and how to interpret the events, issues and actions of key characters.

You will be expected to structure your written work to help others follow your analyses, descriptions and interpretations. A chronological framework is a useful tool because it can make meaning clear by ordering events and helping you to show how you have reached your conclusions. Your historical skills should be supported by your communication skills. Redraft your text to improve its clarity and give it a proof-read to check the grammar, punctuation and spelling.

Topic area 2
Historical sources

Discussion

You will be expected to understand historical events by reading how they were reported at the time. Recent or contemporary history is easier to access because we have the media and a range of other primary sources on which to draw. Sources become fewer as you go further back in time and they are not as easily understood because language has changed over the centuries. Primary sources have a very important role to play in your understanding of history. This understanding will depend on your ability to find the sources and to check things out through speaking, listening, and discussing your ideas with others.

Your tutor or a specialist (like a librarian or the curator of a local museum) will usually be able to help you identify appropriate primary and secondary sources. Ask your questions clearly. Listen carefully to the responses you receive and make a written note of recommended sources. This is particularly important when discussing or seeking advice and help

from someone other than your tutor because there may not be another opportunity to ask them further questions or have a follow-up discussion.

Reading for information

The primary sources you are able to work with will vary according to the period or event you are studying. Primary sources may include:

- Letters written at the time of the event
- Visual records such as wall paintings, carvings and photographs
- Documents such as diaries, official papers and inventories
- Newspaper commentaries, autobiographies and memoirs

Not all primary sources can be taken at face value; always check them for bias and intention.

Where there is a lot of documentary material, you will need to skim for appropriate texts, then scan for factual and other information. Make sure that key points can be substantiated, by cross-referring to information from other sources. Contemporary maps, plans and diagrams can also provide important material and information.

Writing documents

Historical sources can provide sufficient factual information to enable you to produce written text. However, at this level you will be expected to do more than just describe and explain what you have found out. You will be expected to:

- Demonstrate your understanding of causes, consequences and changes
- Analyse key features and characteristics
- Evaluate and select appropriate information from your sources
- Investigate evidence and use it to draw relevant conclusions

The way in which you present your findings and the type of document you produce will vary according to your purpose. Historical essays or reports tend to be either chronological or thematic in structure. Choose a style and a structure that suit your purpose but also help others to follow your ideas and understand your conclusions.

What you must know
Part 1: The Learning Curve will help you with the knowledge you need.

What you must do
Part 2: The Bottom Line will help you with the evidence you need.

Opportunities from course work

Course work provides you with an opportunity to work on a personal project that contributes to your History GCSE. If chosen carefully, this project can also provide evidence for your key skills in communication at levels 1 and 2 because it will provide you with an opportunity to discuss and plan your project with your tutor or in collaboration with others on your programme. It will also enable you to explore information through reading primary and secondary sources and produce a written piece, illustrated and supported by drawings, diagrams or photographs.

Home Economics GCSE

CHILD DEVELOPMENT • CONSUMER STUDIES • TEXTILES
• FOOD AND NUTRITION

About the syllabus

The Home Economics awards help you to develop the knowledge and skills required to organise and manage resources effectively and safely. You will have the opportunity to increase your awareness of the impact of social, cultural and economic factors, as well as your awareness of technological developments, on individuals and groups. You will be expected to apply this knowledge and understanding in order to respond appropriately and effectively to investigations and tasks within the subject.

Topic area 1
Investigating existing resources

An essential skill for home economics is the ability to plan and carry out investigations and tasks that are set by your programme of study. The skills you use will the same for the different aspects of the subject and you will be expected to gather, record, collate, interpret and evaluate evidence. These skills are similar to, and will depend upon, the different aspects of communication: planning, preparing and discussing, reading and obtaining information, and writing documents.

See also: **Hospitality and Catering GNVQ**, page 124.

Discussion

You will be expected to plan and prepare for your investigation. This will involve you in one-to-one discussions with your tutor and group discussions with other people on the programme. The skills you will need include:

- Speaking to others when seeking advice and information
- Listening to others to receive advice or confirm your ideas
- Presenting ideas to others to seek their views
- Selecting images to support, illustrate or explain your ideas

How these skills are applied will depend upon your investigation or task but could be used in:

- **Child development**: when you are collecting first-hand evidence through interviews on the role of the family and its effects on a child's social, emotional and intellectual development.
- **Consumer studies**: when you discuss marketing and advertising techniques with members of a target audience to note impact and influence on consumer choice.
- **Food and nutrition**: when you analyse people's response to food products and the role of availability, sensory characteristics, marketing and advertising, and personal preference.
- **Textiles**: when you find out about new legislation and consumer needs and discuss their effects on the choice of goods and services as well as on quality and costs.

Opportunities

Reading for information

You will be expected to use a range of different sources to help you in your investigation. You will have the opportunity to use a range of primary and secondary sources. Primary sources can include interviews and discussions. Secondary sources include:

- Technical information relevant to the task, such as legislation, scientific data
- Reports and reference materials, such as textbooks, guidance booklets, consumer advice leaflets
- Promotional material produced by manufacturers, marketing organisations, retailers, etc.

You will be expected to use a range of skills, including:

- Identifying and using relevant sources
- Skimming sources to select relevant items
- Scanning relevant text and images for key points
- Classifying information according to its purpose
- Identifying main lines of reasoning
- Producing accessible summaries for future use

Writing documents

Your investigation or task will have to be clearly presented to others. This may be in:

- Oral form (discussed earlier)
- Written form (essay, report, etc.)

When producing written work, make sure your communication skills support the ideas, information and views you are presenting. Your review of your findings should be:

- Structured to help others follow and understand; accuracy, clarity and precision can be achieved by careful use of paragraphs, headings and sub-headings.
- Written in a style that suits the topic; a technical report should use appropriate scientific language and be logically and factually set out.
- Clearly set out to reveal its purpose and conclusions; redraft it to improve clarity and proof-read it to check grammar, punctuation and spelling.
- Illustrated with artwork and mathematics such as photographs and diagrams, charts and graphs, calculations and equations.

Topic area 2
Practical projects

Discussion

You will be expected to use a range of communication skills to undertake your practical work. How they are applied will depend upon the nature of your project. Before discussing the project you will need to explore a range of secondary sources. These will include:

- **Child development:** ideas about sensory exploration and the links between learning and play.
- **Consumer studies:** the choices made by consumers in terms of housing, goods, and services, and links with socio-economic groupings, age and different family groups.
- **Food and nutrition:** food preparation, processing and storage techniques in domestic and commercial production.
- **Textiles:** fibre content and yarn structure, fabric construction and finishes, the characteristics of different textiles.

Once you have a clear appreciation of the necessary information, you can plan and prepare your project then discuss your intentions with your tutor and other people on the programme. This should give you the confidence to produce a series of testable hypotheses to underpin your project.

Reading for information

The sources identified by you and others to assist in planning and preparing for your project will have provided you with a wealth of information. Ensure that you have:

- Separated facts, opinions, and ideas
- Skimmed sources effectively
- Scanned relevant texts for key points
- Identified the information you need
- Made summaries for future use.

Perhaps you are unsure about the accuracy of some information. Try to cross-check it against other sources, particularly if it relates to key project decisions. Legislation is often revised or amended, so check your information is up to date.

Writing documents

A practical project gives you an ideal opportunity to provide written information in a form other than an essay or report. Practical projects that produce an artefact or a final outcome can be supported by a range of different documents, depending on the focus:

- **Child development:** the production of an educational toy intended to stimulate sensory development; this could be supported by a user guide, a technical specification or a production plan.
- **Consumer studies:** the production of a 'good management' guide could use a range of text-based techniques, such as alphabetical order, indexing and cross-referencing, to enable users to search and find relevant information.
- **Food and nutrition:** the production of a special meal or catering event could include menus, recipes or orders of activities and schedules.
- **Textiles:** when producing a textile product, you could produce a

What you must know
Part 1: The Learning Curve will help you with the knowledge you need.

What you must do
Part 2: The Bottom Line will help you with the evidence you need.

technical specification for the fabric, a design for any garment produced, or a leaflet containing information on use and care.

The structure of the material will depend upon the exact role it has to play in clarifying its purpose, promoting its uptake or instructing others on its use.

Irrespective of role, ensure that the form you have chosen, the style of language you have used and the quality of the text you have produced, help others to follow your ideas and understand the purpose of your project.

Information and Communication Technology GCSE

About the syllabus
The ICT award helps you to develop your knowledge, skills and understanding of the role of technology in communicating ideas and information. You will be expected to you find things out using a range of sources such as databases, CD-ROMs and the Internet. You will have the opportunity to use ICT to develop ideas using text, images and numbers. You will also have the opportunity to exchange and share ideas electronically and you will be expected to review, modify and evaluate your work as it progresses.

Topic areas

Your studies for the ICT award will allow you to develop and show the skills of communication in the following general situations:

- Tackling problems using ICT
- Using information sources and ICT tools
- Working with others to explore, develop and pass on information
- Designing information systems
- Evaluating and suggesting improvements to existing systms
- Comparing your own use of ICT with its use in the wider world

Discussion
When using and developing ICT systems you will need to get information about products and techniques. This is a good activity for using your speaking and listening skills. The following activities will help to provide evidence for the key skill:

- Planning and carrying out practical investigations with others
- Sharing ICT resources with other people
- Finding information about firms and their use of ICT
- Discussing and agreeing how to use a system or technique
- Discussing the pros and cons of ICT

- Agreeing safe working procedures

Level 2 expects you to give a short talk or a practical demonstration. The following project areas give good opportunities:

- Explaining features of a system with the help of graphics
- Describing key points about the use of ICT in organisations
- Explaining an aspect of how ICT impacts on people's lives
- Describing how to carry out a particular technique
- Explaining your development work with the help of graphics
- Explaining how to carry out a manufacturing operation
- Describing the features and merits of a new website

Make sure that you support your talk or practical demonstration by using appropriate comments and language adapted to suit your purpose.

Reading for information

When working on assignments and projects you will have many chances to use different types of documents and to choose useful information. Here are some examples:

- Using information on CD-ROMs, databases and the Internet
- Using text, photos and drawings about systems
- Using dictionaries and other explanations of technical terms
- Using databases of product information
- Collecting information about the impact of e-commerce
- Considering the implications of holding personal data
- Browsing websites about organisations and their use of IT
- Consulting software manuals and program listings
- Understanding the logic of an ICT system

Level 2 expects you to show that you can also:

- Make your own decisions about which information to use
- Understand the reason for choices, such as development options
- Make a summary of information you have gathered.

Writing documents

You will need to produce at least two different types of document, and have an image in at least one of them. The following activities will offer good opportunities to show evidence:

- Notes taken during meetings
- Emails sent to other people in a team
- Notes and records of gathering information
- Write-ups of investigation work
- Summaries of development options
- Manuals for a new use of ICT
- Program documentation
- Using spreadsheets
- Inserting graphics into documents
- Essays on ICT in society

The documents must be clear with correct spelling, punctuation and grammar. Although spellcheckers are very useful they aren't perfect so produce rough drafts and proof-read them yourself. Your final documents should be easy to follow so use a good layout with clear headings.

Opportunities from using ICT in other areas

What you must know
Part 1: The Learning Curve will help you with the knowledge you need.

What you must do
Part 2: The Bottom Line will help you with the evidence you need.

Your ICT studies expect you to use information sources and apply ICT tools in other areas of your studies and your life. You are expected to be independent, responsible, effective and reflective about the use of ICT and these qualities match what is needed for the key skills. For example, you may be asked to help friends or people in the community with their information or computer applications. You should record these activities and use this evidence to support your other work in communication. You should also take the opportunities provided by all your work to practise and develop your communication skills and build up your confidence and capabilities.

Mathematics GCSE

About the syllabus
The Mathematics award helps you develop the ability to use and apply mathematics in solving everyday problems, in thinking clearly and in effective communication. To do this you will be expected to have a good understanding of number and algebra, shape and space, measures and data handling. You will have the opportunity to improve your communication skills by:

- Speaking precisely and knowledgeably about mathematical ideas and methods
- Discussing and presenting mathematical ideas and methods, your own and other people's
- Reading and summarising mathematical ideas and methods unambiguously and concisely
- Presenting written information that expresses mathematical ideas and methods precisely and unambiguously

Topic area 1
Using and applying mathematics

Discussion
You will be expected to deal with real problems, simulations or tasks set in a range of contexts. Make sure you understand the purpose of the activity. You can do this by discussing ideas in a one-to-one tutorial with your tutor. This will involve:

- Discussing ideas and methods as you plan your work
- Using mathematical terms to explain your ideas and methods

- Exchanging information and clarifying purpose
- Listening closely and checking you have understood

At level 2 you will also have the opportunity to present your ideas and methods to others. This presentation will involve you in describing ideas mathematically using words, diagrams and symbols in an organised and methodical way so that others can understand and follow your line of reasoning.

Reading for information

You will need to obtain relevant information from a range of sources to enable you to follow lines of enquiry. You will be expected to access a range of different sources and show that you are able to:

- Obtain and compare information to determine and record relevant data
- Skim sources to locate relevant information
- Scan relevant information and collate appropriate data
- Record and summarise data using mathematical language and symbols

Writing documents

As well as presenting your findings using mathematical symbolic notation and explaining your results orally, you will be expected to communicate information and ideas in a written report. This will include mathematical justifications that explain your solutions to problems. These explanations and justifications can be presented as:

- Notes that support your mathematical calculations, including algebraic solutions
- Short evaluation reports that summarise your methods and conclusions
- Annotations to drawings and diagrams used in problems relating to space and shape
- An extended report that explains what you did and suggests future lines of enquiry

Use you communication skills to support your mathematical skills. This requires you to make your meaning clear by choosing your words carefully and using appropriate grammar, punctuation and spelling.

Topic area 2
Handling data

Discussion

Data can be drawn from primary or secondary sources. You will be expected to collect and collate information from a range of different sources, which may present data orally, graphically or textually. You will have the opportunity to collect information orally by:

- Discussing discrete data with your tutor or others
- Conducting interviews with people
- Presenting ideas to others and recording their responses

Make sure you know how to use your discussion, presentation and interviewing skills. Plan thoroughly, speak clearly and choose your words carefully. This will help you to collect information that is relevant, clear and concise.

Reading for information

Secondary sources such as reports, textbooks and magazine articles are also important. Graphical material is a particularly important source of data and statistics. Graphics enable large amounts of data to be presented in a simple and straightforward way.

Look at the focus of graphical material, particularly scales, annotations and captions. This will help you to interpret it accurately. If you are unclear about a graphic, ask someone else to explain it.

Writing documents

Mathematical information and ideas can rarely be presented using text alone. This will give you an opportunity to use other ways of presenting information:

- Line graphs and pie charts
- Histograms and frequency diagrams
- Frequency tables and other tables
- Networks and flow diagrams
- Probability trees
- Matrices, equations and inequalities

Make sure any ideas and solutions are clearly explained as well as mathematically accurate. Label your diagrams, reference your sources and follow appropriate language conventions.

Further opportunities for evidence

Class work activities

Your learning opportunities will provide you with a range of individual tasks that will require you to communicate effectively with others. You will need to:

- Discuss ideas and methods with your tutor and others on your programme
- Present your ideas to others
- Read and summarise information during lessons
- Provide written summaries to support your work

The extent to which these activities could provide valid evidence for the key skill of communication will depend upon how you use and record the evidence you use.

Course work activities

Certain programmes of study use course work as an opportunity to work on a personal project that will contribute to your Mathematics GCSE. If chosen carefully, this project can also provide evidence of your communication skills in the context of mathematics. Make sure that you keep:

- Records of your discussions or presentations
- A bibliography of your sources
- Notes that summarise your findings
- A copy of any final evidence you produce that shows how your written skills have enabled you to communicate your mathematical knowledge, skills and understanding effectively.

Science GCSE
BIOLOGY • CHEMISTRY • PHYSICS

The Science awards help you to develop scientific knowledge and understanding and show you how to apply them to experiments and investigations. You will have the opportunity to develop an understanding of the power of scientific ideas and the limitations of scientific claims. You will be expected to appreciate the technological and environmental applications of science within economic, ethical and social contexts and constraints. Throughout your biology, chemistry and physics programmes you will engage in scientific enquiry. This will provide you with a variety of opportunities to develop, rehearse and apply the skills of communication.

Topic area 1
Experimenting and investigating

Discussion

An essential part of scientific enquiry is your ability to discuss your understanding of scientific knowledge, then plan and prepare to carry out experimental and investigative work. You will need to discuss your plans, ideas and methods with your tutor. This will involve:

- Devising questions that use the correct technical language
- Shaping ideas when you agree methods
- Listening closely to advice you are offered
- Clarifying any points you do not understand
- Moving the conversation forward so that you get the information you need in the time available

At level 2 you will also be expected to make a presentation of your ideas and intentions to others. This may take the form of an oral presentation but it may involve a practical demonstration as you carry out your experiment. Make sure you support your practical demonstration by using appropriate comments and language.

What you must know
Part 1: The Learning Curve will help you with the knowledge you need.

What you must do
Part 2: The Bottom Line will help you with the evidence you need.

See also: **Science GNVQ**, page 148.

Opportunities

Reading for information

Experiments and investigations will be based on information from a range of different sources. You will be expected to read and summarise:

- Relevant scientific information
- Scientific texts and other resources
- Evaluations of other people's science
- Lines of reasoning or methodology presented in scientific information

Writing documents

All experiments and investigations need to be written up. This usually includes the standard conventions of establishing methods, identifying apparatus, recording observations, explaining conclusions and evaluating processes.

You will be expected to support your scientific observations using a range of scientific and technical vocabulary that is accurately spelt and presented using correct grammar and punctuation. Communicate your ideas efficiently and effectively using relevant drawings and diagrams to support your text.

Topic area 2
Observations, ideas and arguments

Discussion

Your programme of study will provide you with the opportunity to explore and communicate the scientific observations, ideas and arguments of others in biology, chemistry and physics. To do this effectively you will need to have discussions with your tutor and other people on your programme.

When preparing for a discussion or making a presentation, you will have the opportunity to use scientific and technical vocabulary and to organise your ideas and language to suit the purpose and situation. Situations may be informal, such as one-to-one discussions with your tutor, or formal, perhaps an organised and structured presentation to an audience. Select information and techniques that are clear and relevant to the situation.

Reading for information

Other people's observations, ideas and arguments may come from several sources, including:

- Technical data in journals and reports
- Chapters and passages in textbooks and reference books
- Research updates on webpages
- Statistics in the media and elsewhere

Skim and scan to find the main lines of reasoning then summarise them for future use.

Writing documents

You will have the opportunity to identify different types of scientific writing when you investigate other people's work. This will help you decide on the form and style you need for your writing. It will depend on what you are doing:

- Reporting on other people's ideas
- Discussing and comparing a range of ideas
- Analysing other peoples arguments and ideas
- Seeking to persuade others

Effective science writing will match form with purpose and put over its meaning in a range of scientific vocabulary following established scientific conventions.

Opportunities from class work activities

You will have a range of opportunities to communicate scientific knowledge and understanding effectively. Here are some of them:

- Discussing ideas and methods with tutors and others
- Presenting your ideas in formal and informal contexts
- Reading a range of different sources, including ICT sources
- Exploring a range of written forms and writing styles

Record these activities and use this evidence to support your other work in communication. Take the opportunities provided by class work to develop your communication skills and build up your confidence.

What you must know
Part 1: The Learning Curve will help you with the knowledge you need.

What you must do
Part 2: The Bottom Line will help you with the evidence you need.

Evidence from GNVQ courses

Art and Design GNVQ
PART ONE • FOUNDATION • INTERMEDIATE

About the specifications
The GNVQ Art and Design awards study topics such as working with materials, using techniques and technology, and exploring other people's work. All are intended to help you develop your own visual language, an important part of communication. You will have the opportunity to see how images combine with speaking, listening, reading and writing to help you communicate accurately and effectively.

See also: **Art GCSE**, page 78.

Topic area 1
Designing and making skills

Discussion
When designing and making things in art, craft and design, consider these questions very carefully:

- What am I making?
- Why am I making it?
- For whom am I making it?

Your thoughts will help you decide on the media, materials, techniques and technology you will need to use. At this level you are unlikely to be able to answer the questions on your own. You will need to know:

- Who to ask about your ideas
- How to prepare your questions
- How to present your questions
- How to show interest
- How to check your understanding
- How to record the main points

As well as discussing ideas at the start of the creative process, your programme of study expects you to present your ideas to others during its development and as part of the evaluation and review process. This is a level 2 key skill and in art, craft and design you should:

- Let your work speak for itself; do not describe

- Describe the ideas behind your work
- Explain your use of materials, techniques and technology
- Use the technical language of art and design correctly
- Be prepared to answer questions
- Listen to others and respond positively

Reading for information

Often the people you ask for advice (your tutors, others on your course or artists, craftspeople and designers) will not be able to answer all your questions. They may suggest that:

- You look at the work of another artist, craftsperson or designer
- You visit a particular gallery or museum
- You read a particular book, magazine, review or catalogue
- You visit a particular website

Reading for information is an important skill, just as research and exploration are central to the creative process.

The visual arts produce an enormous amount of literature on contemporary and historical topics. You need to be able to:

- Skim for relevant and high-quality material
- Scan the material you have selected
- Make appropriate records for later use, e.g.
  - photocopies of images
  - annotated sketches or drawings
  - lists of materials
  - instructions for techniques
  - ideas for your own work

Writing documents

Your programme of study requires you to produce records of investigations into media, materials and associated tools, equipment and technology. The usual records will include:

- Studies
- Test pieces
- Samples
- Models
- Sketchbooks

All are important records of your work and meaningful in different ways. Here are some questions you should ask yourself about your records:

- As they stand, will they be meaningful to others?
- Do they communicate what I have done?
- Do they show what I know and what I can do?

Developmental work is very rarely as meaningful to the spectator or assessor as to the artist, craftsperson or designer. You will need to support your work by a short commentary and annotations to accompany each piece. This commentary could provide:

- A general introduction about what you do
- An index of the different investigations you have conducted
- Descriptions of techniques used, which should be cross-referenced to your work

Use a clear structure to increase the impact and make your meaning clear, include:

- Paragraphs
- Headings and sub-headings
- Bold text
- Numerical references

Proof-read your work and check your grammar, punctuation and spelling. Try to use the technical language of art, craft and design when it is appropriate.

Be prepared to experiment with your communication techniques and remember that your documents should have a purpose, they should be clear and they should be meaningful.

Topic area 2
Exploring other people's work

Your programme of study requires you to produce an exploration of both historical and contemporary art, craft and design work. You will need to:

- Select and compare historical and contemporary work
- Express your own views on other people's work
- Collect and organise your findings
- Present your work to others

This topic provides you with an opportunity to develop and apply all components of the communication key skill and to provide the necessary evidence.

Discussion
You will need to use your speaking and listening skills to identify the focus of your research and then carry out an in-depth study. You may have the opportunity to discuss the selected work with:

- Your tutor
- Others on your programme
- Curators or gallery owners
- Visitors to exhibitions
- Collectors of work
- The artist, craftsperson or designer
- Other artists, craftspeople or designers

In each case you will need to prepare carefully for the discussion or interview. Remember to balance your need for information with the amount of time available to you. This may mean that you prepare different types of questions for different individuals. Always keep records of your discussions.

You may also have the opportunity to make an illustrated presentation of your findings; this will provide evidence for level 2. Make sure you structure your presentation to help your audience follow your line of thinking; do not try to say too much in the time allowed.

Reading for information

The sources available to you will vary according to the contemporary or historical work selected. You may be able to research by:

- Visiting galleries and museums to view their works and read their publications
- Read and summarise reference books or magazine articles
- Access websites or CD-ROMs to obtain information

Try to recognise the intentions behind any writings; here are three things to look at:

- Purpose: a gallery guide is unlikely to be highly critical.
- Style: a newspaper article is likely to be selective and focus on a particular aspect.
- Author: the artist's friends may express views different from the artist's competitors.

If you are aware of a writer's intentions and the main lines of reasoning, you can be more selective in your summaries.

Writing documents

The evidence for your art and design provides you with the opportunity to meet at least one of the evidence requirements of the communication key skill. You can provide either of the following:

- Mounted images with supporting notes (a short document, e.g. a memo)
- An illustrated case study (a long document including an image)

Whichever form your evidence takes, make sure that:

- The structure helps others to understand and follow your research.
- Your style of writing suits your purpose. A factual investigation should be without bias or opinion, whereas a more personal piece of research can include personal views and interpretations.
- Your writing is technically accurate. Follow the rules of grammar, punctuation and spelling; write legibly in handwritten documents.
- Your use of images contributes to other people's understanding of your purpose. This may mean including captions for drawings, annotations to sketches or cross-references to an index or paragraphs.

The quality of your finished evidence will not be determined by the length of your case study but by how clearly and effectively you combine your text with your chosen images.

What you must know
Part 1: The Learning Curve will help you with the knowledge you need.

What you must do
Part 2: The Bottom Line will help you with the evidence you need.

Business GNVQ

See also: **Business Studies GCSE**, page 81; **Retail and Distributive Services**, page 145.

About the specifications

The Business awards investigate a range of businesses to help you understand how they work, how they develop and how they are financed.

Topic area 1
Investigating businesses

Discussion

Your understanding of business, its functions and aims will be based upon the quality of your research. You will have to identify sources of relevant information. You could do this through:

- A one-to-one with your tutor
- Discussions with other people
- Questioning people in your chosen business

You will need to know something about the subject so that you can ask questions on:

- Products and services
- Ownership and management
- Numbers of employees and numbers of sites
- Income, expenditure and profitability
- Share prices for public companies

Some of this information may be sensitive, difficult to explain or difficult to understand. You should be prepared to:

- Adapt what you say or how you speak to suit the situation
- Respond appropriately and ask relevant questions
- Take the lead, move the discussion forward by focusing on a specific area or topic
- Make suitable records for later use

As part of your programme of study you are also expected to make a short oral presentation on one of the areas you have investigated. This is a level 2 key skill; make sure that you:

- Prepare for the talk and clearly understand the topic
- Adapt your presentation to suit your audience
- Organise your information to help your listeners understand it
- Introduce images to support your ideas

Reading for information

Another way to collect information and help you understand your chosen business is to use different written or text-based sources. You will be expected to access a range of different sources, including:

- Company reports and manuals

- Reference books and textbooks
- Newspaper and magazine articles
- Government reports
- Other reports and bulletins
- Websites and CD-ROMs

These sources will help you to collect information on:

- Markets and profitability
- Production and distribution costs
- Wholesale and retail prices
- Location and distribution arrangements
- Investment and finance

You will be expected to:

- Skim your sources to identify relevant texts
- Scan relevant texts to select specific items
- Recognise the intentions behind each item you select
- Identify lines of reasoning that lie within your focus
- Summarise relevant information

Remember that not all information in these sources is text-based. Reading and summarising also refer to collecting information from diagrams, charts, tables and graphs. This is particularly important because information on income, market share and profitability is often presented graphically.

Writing documents

Your programme of study requires you to produce a case study. This does not limit how you present the different types of information you have collected. Always make sure that you:

- Select the form that suits the information, such as text for detailed descriptions or graphical images for organisational charts
- Organise information from different sources so it is consistent in terms of format and layout
- Use technical vocabulary when appropriate, such as when describing aims, objectives and organisational structure
- Make your meaning clear by using accurate grammar, punctuation and spelling

Your case study is likely to provide you with evidence of an extended piece of writing, and inclusion of graphs, tables and charts will meet the key skill requirement on image at this level.

Topic area 2
Enterprise and financial literacy

You will be expected to show your awareness of the role played by finance in business activity. Here are some areas to investigate:

- Accounts available to borrowers
- How to borrow money
- How to get the best deal when borrowing
- The responsibilities of the borrower

Discussion

To obtain information on finance you may find it helpful to discuss your needs with:

- Your tutor
- Your friends and family
- A building society or bank
- A financial adviser.

Make sure that you:

- Prepare questions to structure your discussions
- Seek clarification until you get clear answers
- Recognise the other person's intentions
- Obtain answers to all important questions

Your programme of study describes a presentation as a group exercise. You may be required to report back to others on your findings. This is a level 2 key skill; make sure that you:

- Fully understand what you intend to say and have notes, overhead transparencies or other aids to prompt and guide you
- Explain your findings to the group; try to use examples or amounts that are relevant to your topic
- Structure your talk so that it is clear and logical
- Use tables or diagrams to make technical or difficult points easier to understand.

Reading for information

As part of your investigation into sources of funding, you will be expected to read a range of relevant information. You are also expected to develop an understanding of the means by which payments are made in business.

Understanding business documentation is an important part of this topic. You will need to be able to read, understand and differentiate between:

- Contractual documents
- Invoices for materials or services
- Bills of sale
- Receipts
- Purchase documents
- Wages and salary costs

You may also be required to select and summarise relevant information from these documents as well as explain the role each plays in effective business practices.

Writing documents

This topic requires you to produce a business plan and it provides you with an opportunity to produce an extended document that includes written text, graphical images and financial data.

Make sure the layout you choose suits your purpose and provides a clear link between these different forms of information. The final form will depend upon how you decide to present your evidence. A case study approach will produce a complex document. A presentation will require you to prepare overhead transparencies or a PowerPoint presentation; this may include:

- Simple bullet points to describe the business
- A diagram of products, services and customers
- A table of resources needed
- A chart or spreadsheet including start-up and running costs
- A spreadsheet of income, expenditure and profit
- A list of available resources and their costs
- A diagram for purchasing items
- Examples of business documents

Make sure that your written work is clear and accurate and suits the purpose of your presentation. Do not put too much text on each transparency and make sure it can be read and understood by everyone.

Opportunities from optional units

All units of the Business GNVQ will require you to develop and apply your communication skills. You will need to decide when it is appropriate to generate specific key skill evidence.

Construction and the Built Environment GNVQ

PART ONE • FOUNDATION • INTERMEDIATE

About the specifications

The Construction and Built Environment awards study topics like towns and cities, how buildings are designed and built, what materials and methods are used. The optional units include building design, construction processes, civil engineering, building services and town planning.

Topic areas

Communicating is important when studying and working in construction and the built environment. Here are some typical areas for showing your communication skills:

- Investigations into local areas and buildings

What you must know
Part 1: The Learning Curve will help you with the knowledge you need.

What you must do
Part 2: The Bottom Line will help you with the evidence you need.

Opportunities

- Design procedures
- Properties and uses of construction materials
- Techniques used in construction and building services

Discussion

To investigate the features of your local area and its buildings you will first need to get information, so this is a good activity for using your speaking and listening skills. Here are some activities to help you produce evidence for the key skill:

- Planning and making site visits
- Planning and carrying out practical investigations
- Using measuring equipment and IT resources
- Finding text and photos about town features
- Choosing materials and tools for a job
- Discussing client needs in a design brief
- Discussing material properties and how to use them
- Choosing materials to meet a budget
- Agreeing how a job is to be carried out
- Agreeing safe working procedures

You need to show that you can say things which are clear and which suit the situation. Your subject has many technical terms and you should show that you can use the right ones for your project. Remember to show that you can listen carefully to other people.

Level 2 expects you to give a short talk. The following areas may be good opportunities:

- Explaining features on photos and drawings of buildings and towns
- Explaining key points on schedules of operations
- Explaining data from your tests on materials, e.g. on bar charts
- Explaining your design work using drawings and other graphics
- Explaining how to carry out a construction operation

Reading for information

When working on projects in construction and the built environment you will have many chances to use different documents and to choose useful information. Here are some examples:

- Using maps, plans and drawings stored electronically
- Using text and photos about town features
- Using dictionary definitions of technical terms
- Using data on strength and other material properties
- Using information about costs
- Understanding the sequence of jobs in a project

Level 2 expects you to show that you can also:

- Make your own choices of information
- Understand the reason for choices, such as in design
- Summarise information you have gathered

Writing documents

You will need to produce at least two different types of document, one with an image, and the following activities will offer good opportunities for evidence:

- Notes taken during meetings
- Emails to other people in your team
- Letters, memos and other correspondence
- Notes and records of site visits
- Write-ups of laboratory work
- Design drawings with titles and labels
- Summaries of design options
- Records of working through calculations
- Spreadsheets printouts plus graphs or charts

The documents must be clear with correct spelling, punctuation and grammar. Spellcheckers on computers are very useful but they aren't perfect, so produce several sets of rough drafts for careful checking. Your final documents should be easy to follow, so use a good layout with clear headings.

What you must know
Part 1: The Learning Curve will help you with the knowledge you need.

What you must do
Part 2: The Bottom Line will help you with the evidence you need.

Engineering GNVQ
PART ONE • FOUNDATION • INTERMEDIATE

About the specifications

The topics in the Engineering awards include engineering design and drawing, investigating the workings of modern engineering products and the making of a product. The optional units offer further studies such as engineering maths and science, computing, automation and engineering servicing.

Topic areas

While studying or working in engineering you get many opportunities to use communication skills and these can be found in the following major areas of the GNVQs:

- Investigating new technology products
- Design processes
- Making products
- Technology and science

Discussion

To investigate engineering products, processes and technology you will need to gather information, so this is a good activity for using your speaking and listening skills. Here are some activities to help you produce evidence for the key skill:

- Working in a team to collect information
- Planning and carrying out practical investigations

See also: **Design and Technology GCSE**, page 85; **Manufacturing GNVQ**, page 136.

Opportunities

- Using measuring equipment and IT resources
- Using text and photos in information about firms
- Using text and photos in information about products
- Choosing materials and tools for a job
- Discussing client needs in a design brief
- Discussing material properties and how to use them
- Choosing materials to meet a budget
- Agreeing how a process is to be carried out
- Setting up engineering tools and machinery
- Agreeing safe working procedures

Level 2 expects you to give a short talk. The following areas may be good opportunities:

- Explaining features about products using photos and drawings
- Describing key points about engineering processes
- Describing the scientific principles of a product or service
- Explaining your engineering calculations
- Explaining your design work with the help of graphics
- Explaining how to use engineering tools or machinery

Reading for information

When working on assignments and projects in engineering you will have many chances to use different types of documents and to choose information. Here are some examples:

- Using technical drawings on CD-ROMs, databases and the websites
- Using text, photos and drawings about products
- Using dictionary definitions of technical terms
- Using databases of manufacturers' data
- Using databases and graphs of performance data
- Consulting on-screen drawings, production plans and service schedules
- Looking up sizes and qualities of materials in databases
- Setting up electronic equipment with new scales and settings
- Using information about equipment and processes such as CAD

Level 2 expects you to show that you can also:

- Make your own choices of information
- Understand the reason for choices
- Summarise information you have gathered

Writing documents

You will need to produce at least two different types of document, one with an image, and the following activities will offer good opportunities for evidence:

- Notes taken during meetings
- Emails to other people in your team
- Letters, memos and other correspondence

- Notes and records of visits to firms
- Write-ups of investigation work
- Design drawings with titles and labels
- Summaries of design options
- Records of engineering calculations
- Spreadsheet graphs to compare figures
- Inserting graphics into documents

The documents must be clear with correct spelling, punctuation and grammar. Spellcheckers on computers are very useful but they aren't perfect, so produce several sets of rough drafts for careful checking. Your final documents should be easy to follow, so use a good layout with clear headings.

What you must know
Part 1: The Learning Curve will help you with the knowledge you need.

What you must do
Part 2: The Bottom Line will help you with the evidence you need.

Health and Social Care GNVQ
PART ONE • FOUNDATION • INTERMEDIATE

About the specifications
The Health and Social Care awards study topics such as investigating the sector, promoting health and well-being, and personal development and relationships.

Topic area 1
Health and well-being

This topic is about:

- People's needs for health and well-being
- Looking at lifestyles
- Considering experiences and feelings
- Identifying health and well-being needs
- Preparing a plan to improve the situation.

The range of activities necessary to meet the requirements of this topic should provide ample opportunity for you to develop all aspects of your communication key skill.

Discussion
You should have a clear understanding of all aspects of good health in general before being able to identify the health and well-being needs of your target individual or group. This will provide you with opportunities to find out about health and well-being through discussions with:

- Your tutors
- Other people on your programme
- Specialist doctors, nurses, etc.
- At-risk groups and their representatives

To gain the most from your discussions you should be clear about:

- What is meant by health and well-being

EVIDENCE FROM GNVQ COURSES | **121**

- The people or groups that interest you
- How to ask follow-up questions
- When to move the discussion forward
- How to cover all your questions in the time
- How you will record your information

Before presenting your final plan you may have an opportunity to talk through your ideas with others. So that you can use this experience to refine your plan, you should try to make your presentation or talk as focused as possible. This will provide level 2 key skill evidence and will involve:

- Bringing your ideas together and preparing notes or visual aids
- Using technical language to make your meaning unambiguous
- Organising your information so it is logical and clear to others
- Giving clear signals when you are moving from point to point

Reading for information

It is unlikely that the discussions you have with others will provide you with all the information or details you require. You will be expected to access a range of different text-based sources of relevant information. These will include:

- Health promotion leaflets
- Newspaper and magazine articles
- Government or agency reports

The style, layout and nature of these documents will vary according to:

- The topic, such as diet or housing
- The audience, such as specialists or target group
- The focus or intentions, such as information or promotion
- The author, such as the government or a charity

You will need to skim for appropriate texts then scan for relevant information. Be aware of the writer's intentions because this can affect the relevance or quality of the information provided. If you are unsure, try to check a writer's accuracy by seeking other people's work on the same topic.

Writing documents

Having summarised, sifted and sorted, you can begin to develop a health plan by combining your information drawn from different sources. You should use:

- **Written information**: to identify factors that affect the health and well-being of your chosen person or group.
- **Graphical material**: to help others, including your chosen person or group, understand the targets you have set.
- **Charts and tables**: to show the benefits of using the health plan or to set out a schedule of events to implement the plan successfully.

You should decide how your plan should be presented. It may be presented orally and supported by a short set of notes, charts or diagrams. The plan may also be presented as an extended illustrated document that uses the images suggested above to help explain the details of the plan, its targets and how health and well-being can be achieved.

The final form and layout of your plan should be decided by you as you consider how best to communicate with your chosen person or group. Its form should vary according to the age, ability and literacy skills of your chosen person or group. Whichever form you choose, always be accurate, clear and straightforward. Remember that the main aim is to communicate, not confuse.

Topic area 2
Research in health and social care

To carry out a research project you will need to find and use different sources and types of information. These will include:

- **Primary sources (discussion and talking)**: information you collect by making observations, asking questions or conducting a survey.
- **Secondary sources (reading and summarising)**: information drawn from textbooks, reports, promotional material or statistical data; IT sources such as CD-ROMs and the Internet.

You must decide which sources are likely to provide you with the most relevant information. The clearer you are about what you are looking for, the more easily you are likely to identify appropriate sources and select relevant information.

Discussion
When you collect information from primary sources through questioning:

- Standardise your approach to questioning
- Make your questions clear and unambiguous
- Ask questions that will elicit relevant information
- Consider open and closed questions and other sorts

If consistency is important you may decide to produce a questionnaire.

Another way of collecting primary information is through a presentation or short talk to a group. This is a level 2 key skill; you will need to be clear about:

- What you wish to communicate
- What you want the outcome to be
- How you intend to record what is said
- How you can keep to the subject

Keep careful records of the numbers of people involved and the nature of the audience.

Reading for information
The range of secondary sources available to you should include:

- Textbook information
- Recent research documents
- Articles from newspapers or magazines
- Up-to-date information via the Internet

Collect these three types of information; make sure you know the difference between them.

- Background details
- Relevant facts or data
- Attitudes, ideas and opinions

Your communication skills will help you to:

- Sift and sort relevant information
- Recognise a writer's intentions
- Identify the main lines of reasoning
- Summarise information that meets your purpose

Once you have collected all the information you need, you should analyse your notes carefully then:

- Discard information that is too biased, irrelevant or of poor quality
- Consider the best way to present your findings and conclusions

Writing documents

The effectiveness of your research will be determined by your ability to communicate your findings to others. This is why the communication key skill is so important. The written form you choose will depend upon the nature of your research. You may prepare:

- Short items to go with diagrams
- A set of OHTs
- An illustrated essay
- A detailed technical report

What you must know
Part 1: The Learning Curve will help you with the knowledge you need.

What you must do
Part 2: The Bottom Line will help you with the evidence you need.

Whichever form you choose, you must make every effort to ensure that the structure and style suit your research. Make sure, also, that you proof read all written text for accuracy of grammar, punctuation and spelling.

Opportunities from optional units

All units of the Health and Social Care GNVQs will require you to develop and apply your communication skills. You will need to decide when it is appropriate to generate specific key skill evidence.

Hospitality and Catering GNVQ
PART ONE • FOUNDATION • INTERMEDIATE

About the specifications
The Hospitality and Catering awards study food and drink, accommo-

dation and front of office, and practical investigations into hospitality and catering outlets and industries. There will be some opportunities for you to specialise in aspects of hospitality and catering that interest you. All units will give you an opportunity to generate components of the communication key skill evidence.

Topic area 1
Investigations into industries or outlets

See also: **Home Economics GCSE**, page 99

You will be expected to identify suitable sources of information for your investigation. You will need to know:

- Where to look for information
- How to collect information
- How to sort the information you collect

You will be searching for information on:

- The size and scope of the industry
- The income and profit it generates
- Size of the labour force and roles of employees
- Industry trends in recent reports

You will be expected to use primary sources and secondary sources.

Discussion

A primary source is direct observation and discussion with people who work in the industry – people employed in outlets, tourist information offices and libraries. You are expected to interview at least one person who carries out hospitality-related activities and at least one who carries out catering-related activities. To do this effectively you must:

- Use appropriate hospitality and catering terms
- Prepare suitable questions
- Adapt your questions to suit the situation and the professional rank of the person you are interviewing
- Record information so it is accessible and usable

At level 2 you will also have the opportunity to present your findings to others and to discuss your ideas and findings. Prepare properly by making notes or using other aids to help you:

- Explain your findings using the correct terms
- Structure your talk to help others contribute
- Respond to ideas and record them for the future

Reading for information

The secondary sources available to you will vary but they include:

- Publicity brochures and leaflets
- Guides and handbooks
- Telephone directories and other reference sources

- Statistics compiled by government and industry
- Information on CD-ROMs or websites

You are expected to:

- Skim sources to identify useful texts
- Scan texts to find useful information
- Recognise the intentions behind text
- Use relevant pictures, charts and diagrams

Writing documents

The size and diversity of the industry have led to huge amounts of published information. Be clear about your purpose as you sort, sift, combine and prepare your results. You must also be clear about how to select and present this information; your choice of structure and style will determine the quality of your presentation.

Your investigation into hospitality and catering will give you the opportunity to produce an extended document that combines:

- Written text on products, services and characteristics of outlets
- Diagrams and charts that relate work routines to staffing structures
- Lists or spreadsheets to show industry size in your chosen locality

Redraft your work until it's clear and reads well. Proof-read your work to check its grammar, punctuation and spelling.

Topic area 2
Investigating accommodation and front office services

Front office services are essentially about choosing and using the full range of communication skills in an appropriate way and at an appropriate time. Front office skills include:

- Answering the telephone and taking reservations
- Handling post, filing papers and customer records
- Receiving and registering customers on arrival
- Handling enquiries and requests
- Dealing with customer bills and payments

The skills you need to identify for different situations include:

- Speaking and listening
- Observing
- Writing
- Showing

These may refer to communications with one customer or a group of customers.

Discussion

Your investigation and related activities require you to:

- Demonstrate at least three different reception activities and two different sources of information
- Present information on cleaning and servicing one accommodation area

You should choose at least one front office industry that allows you to discuss with customers and provide them with information. This could include:

- Booking in or checking out. Make sure that you ask for information clearly and listen carefully to the response. Also make sure that all paperwork is completed accurately and filed or stored carefully.
- Responding to a telephone enquiry. Make sure that you listen carefully and respond appropriately using all the appropriate conventions for beginning and ending telephone conversations.
- Advising a group of customers or visitors on the location of a local tourist attraction. This may involve using maps, diagrams, timetables and arranging block bookings.

Your presentation on cleaning and servicing an accommodation area may be in the form of a short talk to other people on your programme. This is a level 2 key skill and should include:

- An explanation of the links between front office and accommodation
- Arrangements for cleaning and serving all outlets
- How staff clean and service different aspects of accommodation
- The importance of health, safety and security arrangements

Reading for information
Besides observing you will need to add to your knowledge and understanding by reading a range of different sources for relevant information. These will include:

- Brochures and publicity leaflets to identify suitable outlets
- Booklets and training manuals on front office activities
- In-house rules and regulations about managing arrangements
- Specifications, including qualifications for workers in the industry
- Manuals on safety, hygiene and security procedures

You will need to be able to identify, extract and summarise the information you seek out and decide how relevant it is to your investigation.

Writing documents
This topic does not require you to produce a case study or an extended essay or report. However, you are required to produce records of your investigation. These records may comprise:

- A series of notes and images linked by an index system
- A short written report that introduces individual items
- A series of OHTs or PowerPoint slides
- A set of handouts for an oral presentation

What you must know
Part 1: The Learning Curve will help you with the knowledge you need.

What you must do
Part 2: The Bottom Line will help you with the evidence you need.

Opportunities

Whichever method you choose to record your findings, make sure that:

- Your content is relevant
- Your method is appropriate
- Your information is clear and accurate

Information and Communication Technology GNVQ

PART ONE • FOUNDATION • INTERMEDIATE

About the specifications

The ICT award helps you to develop your knowledge, skills and understanding of the role of technology in communicating ideas and information. You will be expected to you find things out using a range of sources such as databases, CD-ROMs and the Internet. You will have the opportunity to use ICT to develop ideas using text, images and numbers. You will also have the opportunity to exchange and share ideas electronically and you will be expected to review, modify and evaluate your work as it progresses.

Topic areas

Your studies for the ICT award will allow you to develop and show the skills of communication in the following general situations:

- Tackling problems using ICT
- Using information sources and ICT tools
- Working with others to explore, develop and pass on information
- Designing information systems
- Evaluating and suggesting improvements to existing systms
- Comparing your own use of ICT with its use in the wider world

Discussion

When using and developing ICT systems you will need to get information about products and techniques. This is a good activity for using your speaking and listening skills. The following activities will help to provide evidence for the key skill:

- Planning and carrying out practical investigations with others
- Sharing ICT resources with other people
- Finding information about firms and their use of ICT
- Discussing and agreeing how to use a system or technique
- Discussing the pros and cons of ICT
- Agreeing safe working procedures

Level 2 expects you to give a short talk or a practical demonstration. The following project areas give good opportunities:

- Explaining features of a system with the help of graphics
- Describing key points about the use of ICT in organisations
- Explaining an aspect of how ICT impacts on people's lives
- Describing how to carry out a particular technique
- Explaining your development work with the help of graphics
- Explaining how to carry out a manufacturing operation
- Describing the features and merits of a new website

Make sure that you support your talk or practical demonstration by using appropriate comments and language adapted to suit your purpose.

Reading for information

When working on assignments and projects you will have many chances to use different types of documents and to choose useful information. Here are some examples:

- Using information on CD-ROMs, databases and the Internet
- Using text, photos and drawings about systems
- Using dictionaries and other explanations of technical terms
- Using databases of product information
- Collecting information about the impact of e-commerce
- Considering the implications of gathering and holding personal data
- Browsing websites about organisations and their use of IT
- Consulting software manuals and program listings
- Understanding the logic of an ICT system

Level 2 expects you to show that you can also:

- Make your own decisions about which information to use
- Understand the reason for choices, such as development options
- Make a summary of information you have gathered.

Writing documents

You will need to produce at least two different types of document, and have an image in at least one of them. The following activities will offer good opportunities to show evidence:

- Notes taken during meetings
- Emails sent to other people in a team
- Notes and records of gathering information
- Write-ups of investigation work
- Summaries of development options
- Manuals for a new use of ICT
- Program documentation
- Using spreadsheets
- Inserting graphics into documents
- Essays on ICT in society

The documents must be clear with correct spelling, punctuation and grammar. Although spellcheckers are very useful they aren't perfect so produce

What you must know
Part 1: The Learning Curve will help you with the knowledge you need.

What you must do
Part 2: The Bottom Line will help you with the evidence you need.

rough drafts and proof-read them yourself. Your final documents should be easy to follow so use a good layout with clear headings.

Opportunities from using ICT in other areas

Your ICT studies expect you to use information sources and apply ICT tools in other areas of your studies and your life. You are expected to be independent, responsible, effective and reflective about the use of ICT and these qualities match what is needed for the key skills. For example, you may be asked to help friends or people in the community with their information or computer applications. You should record these activities and use this evidence to support your other work in communication. You should also take the opportunities provided by all your work to practise and develop your communication skills and build up your confidence and capabilities.

Land and Environment GNVQ

PART ONE • FOUNDATION • INTERMEDIATE

About the specifications

The Land and Environment awards study topics such as caring for animals and plants, investigating environmental factors, and investigating the land and environment sector.

Topic area 1
Investigating the land and environment sector

When investigating the factors that influence the location of business organisations you are expected to produce a report that:

- Explains why your chosen business is located in a particular area
- Describes the enterprises operated by your chosen business
- Describes the husbandry or production methods used
- Describes the resources required and how they are used
- Explains the contribution made by your chosen business to the local area
- Describes the job roles

To investigate successfully and report your findings effectively, you will need to use the full range of communication skills.

Discussion

You will have the opportunity to discuss job roles with those working in your chosen business organisation. The information they can give you will be very important to your final report but their own communication skills may vary according to their particular job role. This means that you must prepare for each interview by:

- Deciding what type of information you are seeking

- Adapting your questions to suit the situation and the professional rank of the person you are interviewing
- Learning and using the technical vocabulary appropriately
- Preparing supplementary questions to manage the interview
- Knowing how you will record the information you obtain

You will have the opportunity to give a short talk to others on what you have found out; this will provide evidence for the level 2 key skill. If this happens before you complete your final report, use it to:

- Test out the accuracy of information about your chosen business
- Explore how to describe your findings on enterprises and resources
- Seek others' views on how your business influences the local area
- Try out structures and language that help your audience to follow your line of thought

Reading for information

You are unlikely to be able to find out everything you need by speaking and listening to others. To enable your report to meet the topic requirements you will need to use correct and accurate information, so you will need to access a range of written sources, including:

- Government and National Farmers' Union (NFU) reports on land use in the UK
- Company reports and magazine articles on finance and employment
- National and local newspapers for local angles on changing land use

Each type of document will provide information that will need to be sorted and sifted. You will need to decide whether information is:

- Relevant
- Accurate
- An opinion
- Appropriate

Writing documents

You will have the opportunity to develop your writing skills by producing a range of different documents. These will include:

- Letters to your chosen business
- Memos to potential interviewees
- Notes of your discussions or interviews
- Summaries of documents you have read
- Extended coverage of your main findings

You will need to decide which of these written documents can be used as evidence of your communication skills and which can be used to support your finished report.

Try to use different styles and structures that are appropriate to each task;

- Notes and summaries could use headings, sub-headings and bullets
- Longer text should use technical vocabulary and short paragraphs

Topic area 2
Caring for plants and animals

Discussion

There are obviously differences in the care of plants and animals at this level but your discussions and conversations will probaby be very similar. You should discuss your choice of plant species and propagation methods or your choice of animal species and breeding methods with your tutor or a professional you are working with.

You will need to use your speaking and listening skills throughout your work. You should:

- Check that you understand the plant or animal species
- Check that you understand the breeding or propagation method
- Learn when to ask questions and when to listen attentively
- Show that you have understood instructions by giving appropriate responses
- Confirm you are doing the correct things to care for animals or plants
- Use appropriate technical vocabulary in a variety of different situations

Reading for information

You should build upon your practical experience by researching and reading about your chosen topic. This information will come from a range of sources:

- Technical manuals
- Textbooks
- Research reports
- Magazines and websites

Check your understanding by discussing your findings with other people. Always summarise the information you collect; produce clear summaries that will make sense in the future.

Writing documents

Your records should include a range of information:

- A daily log that includes your observations and data
- Notes on genetic principles plus a few worked examples
- Descriptions of husbandry methods used and care you have provided

You will be expected to produce some records on-site, others may be written up later. It is acceptable for you to use different styles and structures to reflect the different circumstances in which you are writing. However, in each case your communication must be accurate, clear and suit its purpose.

What you must know
Part 1: The Learning Curve will help you with the knowledge you need.

What you must do
Part 2: The Bottom Line will help you with the evidence you need.

Leisure and Tourism GNVQ

PART ONE • FOUNDATION • INTERMEDIATE

About the specifications

The Leisure and Tourism awards study topics such as investigating leisure and tourism sectors and marketing and promotion.

Topic area 1
Investigating leisure and tourism sectors

See also: **Geography GCSE**, page 92

The leisure and tourism sectors are made up of many different facilities and organisations, from leisure centres and theatres to travel agents and airlines. Your investigation into the role the sectors play in today's society will provide you with a range of opportunities to develop and demonstrate your communication key skills.

Discussion

Discuss these issues with your tutor and other people:

- Your understanding of leisure and tourism
- The links between leisure and tourism
- Which area you are going to investigate
- Facilities and organisations in your chosen area.

These discussions will provide the basis for your investigations, so you should make sure that you:

- Express your ideas and opinions clearly
- Take care over what you say and how you say it
- Listen carefully to other people's contributions
- Note down useful comments or helpful suggestions
- Check you understand what other people say
- Get what you need from any discussions, perhaps by preparing questions

You may also be asked to lead a group or give a short talk to update others on your progress. This is a level 2 key skill. To get the most out of this opportunity, make sure that you have:

- Carried out research and have something to present
- Prepared some aids such as notes, diagrams or graphs
- Structured your talk to help others follow it

Other opportunities for you to practice your speaking and listening skills may come from interviews with people working in the industry. Prepare well and know what questions you are going to ask. Remember that your interviewees are busy people who are trying to help you.

Reading for information

You will not be able to collect all the information you need through talking to others. You will need to use text-based sources as well. These should include:

- Textbooks and CD-ROMs on leisure and tourism
- Government and industry reports on the sector
- Guidebooks from The National Trust, English Heritage, etc.
- Brochures and leaflets from tourist information offices

You should identify:

- Links between different leisure and tourism operations

- Details of individual leisure and tourism industries
- The activities and facilities provided by each operation
- The number of people employed in the sectors
- The contribution to the economy of your chosen area

You are likely to find more sources of information than you need; you should therefore:

- Skim to locate relevant sources
- Scan to extract useful information
- Sort into fact, opinion and description
- Select any diagrams, charts or graphs
- Produce a summary for your investigation

Writing documents

Your investigation will produce a range of written information including:

- Notes of discussions
- Summaries of texts
- Letters and memos
- Explanations of key points
- Annotated diagrams or charts

Your topic does not require you to produce a written essay or a final report. You could use the written information you have collected to produce an extended investigation with illustrations:

- Produce an index that links each one of your written pieces
- Structure your document using appropriate heading levels
- Redraft individual documents to fit your purpose better
- Introduce appropriate technical language
- Use maps, graphs or charts to emphasise or clarify

Topic area 2
Marketing and promotion

Leisure and tourism organisations will survive only if people know about them and what they have to offer. Traditionally, marketing and promotion have been achieved through:

- Advertisements
- Brochures and leaflets
- Posters and point-of-sale items
- Merchandising materials
- Videos
- Press releases

This topic offers you the opportunity to seek and use a range of sources to investigate marketing activities and the production of promotional material.

Discussion

An important aspect of market research is direct contact with customers or potential customers. Most organisations do this through personal or telephone surveys. If you participate in a survey you must:

- Explain yourself carefully and ask your questions clearly
- Change your manner to suit the situation and the person you are interviewing
- Listen carefully and check you have understood
- Check that you have obtained a genuine response and valid evidence
- Cover all the questions and complete the survey
- Be civil and polite at all times

Another aspect of marketing is promotion. You may have an opportunity to contribute to one of these activities:

- Public relations exercise
- Demonstration or display
- Sales promotion exercise

You may then need to give a short talk explaining the products and services you are promoting. This will provide evidence for the level 2 key skill because you will be trying to persuade people to buy or use them. You should:

- Prepare fully by identifying your target audience
- Choose your words to suit the promotion
- Cover all the points clearly, effectively and briefly
- Use images or other aids such as photographs or videos
- Involve your audience through questions or other devices

Reading for information

You are required to:

- Identify and describe the product or place, the price and promotion
- Demonstrate a clear understanding of marketing language
- Produce an item of promotional material

To do this effectively you will need to:

- Identify and read a range of industry sources
- Make notes from more technical documents
- Collect and review promotional materials

Make sure that:

- The information you collect is authentic, useful and valid
- The notes, summaries or examples can be used later on

Writing documents

The quality of your findings will depend upon how you collate, organise and present your different pieces of evidence. Your structure and style should effectively combine your factual information with your personal descriptions.

What you must know
Part 1: The Learning Curve will help you with the knowledge you need.

What you must do
Part 2: The Bottom Line will help you with the evidence you need.

EVIDENCE FROM GNVQ COURSES | **135**

The requirement to produce a piece of promotional material gives you the opportunity to use a different style of writing that may include:

- Photographs, drawings, charts and tables
- Text of different font sizes and types
- A variety of formats and layouts

Whichever style you use, make sure your meaning is clear and your grammar, punctuation and spelling are accurate.

Manufacturing GNVQ

PART ONE • FOUNDATION • INTERMEDIATE

About the specification

The Manufacturing awards investigate how companies use new technology to make products. In other units you develop your skills for designing and making products. The optional units give you a choice of further studies in manufacturing, including computing, automation and quality control.

Topic areas

See also: **Engineering GNVQ**, page 119; **Design and Technology GCSE**, page 85.

While studying and working in manufacturing you get many opportunities to use communication skills in the following major areas:

- Investigating technology and produces
- Working with a design brief
- Design processes
- Making a product

Discussion

To investigate modern manufacturing you will need to get information about products and companies, so this is a good activity for using your speaking and listening skills. Here are some activities to help you produce evidence for the key skill.

- Planning and making visits to firms
- Planning and carrying out practical investigations
- Using measuring equipment and IT resources
- Using text and photos in information about firms
- Using text and photos in information about products
- Choosing materials and tools for a job
- Discussing client needs in a design brief
- Discussing material properties and how to use them
- Choosing materials to meet a budget
- Agreeing how a process is to be carried out
- Agreeing safe working procedures

Level 2 expects you to give a short talk. The following areas may be good opportunities:

- Explaining features about products using photos and drawings

- Describing key points about firms and organisations
- Describing the features of manufacturing operations
- Describing how a product works
- Explaining your design work using drawings and other graphics
- Explaining how to carry out a manufacturing operation

Reading for information

When working on assignments and projects in manufacturing you will have many chances to use different types of documents and to choose useful information. Here are some examples:

- Using technical drawings on CD-ROMs, databases and websites
- Using text, photos and drawings about products
- Using dictionaries and other explanations of technical terms
- Using databases of manufacturers' data
- Using databases and graphs of performance data
- Consulting on-screen drawings, production plans and service schedules
- Looking up sizes and qualities of materials in databases
- Setting up electronic equipment with new scales and settings
- Using information about processes
- Creating a sequence from several manufacturing stages

Level 2 expects you to show that you can also:

- Make your own choices of information
- Understand the reason for choices
- Summarise information you have gathered

Writing documents

You will need to produce at least two different types of document, one with an image, and the following activities will offer good opportunities for evidence:

- Notes taken during meetings
- Emails sent to other people in your team
- Letters, memos and other correspondence
- Notes and records of visits to firms
- Write-ups of investigation work
- Design drawings with titles and labels
- Summaries of design options
- Records of working through calculations
- Spreadsheet graphs to compare figures
- Inserting graphics into documents

The documents must be clear with correct spelling, punctuation and grammar. Spellcheckers on computers are very useful but they aren't perfect, so produce several sets of rough drafts for careful checking. Your final documents should be easy to follow so use a good layout with clear headings.

What you must know
Part 1: The Learning Curve will help you with the knowledge you need.

What you must do
Part 2: The Bottom Line will help you with the evidence you need.

Opportunities

Media: Communication and Production GNVQ

About the specifications

The Media awards include the development of investigative and production skills. Communication skills are also a central dimension. You will need to choose skills that are relevant to different topics and meet the assessment requirements of the key skill at a specified level.

Topic area 1
Investigating media industries and products

The media industry is large and diverse, ranging from traditional text-based communications to the latest interactive digital communications technology. Any investigation will give you the opportunity to collect relevant information from a range of sources using all the communication skills.

Discussion

As this industry is large and diverse it is likely that different people on your programme will investigate different sectors, their media products and the range of employment opportunities. You can develop your oral skills by:

- Discussing the industry's make-up and its product range
- Discussing the range of jobs in the sector you investigate
- Taking part in a group discussion on the media in society
- Giving a short talk to others on a media job or a media role
- Giving a presentation on:
  - communication techniques in your sector
  - how your sector captures audience attention
  - contributions made by new technologies

For each of the above opportunities you should:

- Be clear about what you will say and have all your aids ready
- Use relevant technical terms to describe the industry
- Adapt your presentations to suit your audiences
- Make effective use of graphs and charts, tables and diagrams

Whichever style or structure you use, be clear and accurate, especially over grammar, punctuation and spelling.

Reading for information

The media industry produces a range of products and materials that inform and promote its different sectors. These products and materials include:

- Journals, newspapers, magazines and periodicals
- Annual reports and careers literature
- Marketing or market research literature
- Company brochures, films, photographs, reports and videos
- Online websites and offline CD-ROMs

You will be expected to read and analyse these different sources so you can demonstrate your understanding of the media industry, including:

- The products of different sectors
- The different employment roles
- Marketing and market research techniques
- Bias and opinion in the media
- The impact of technology

These sources are so diverse that you must develop and apply a range of reading techniques, including:

- Skimming for appropriate content
- Scanning for details and relevance
- Pulling out relevant facts, descriptions or opinions
- Identifying relevant images
- Summarising findings for future use

Writing documents

This topic does not require written evidence and could, if required, be achieved through an oral presentation. Note that even a short talk or presentation requires written notes and other aids. Whichever method you choose to present your evidence, make sure that all written material is:

- Relevant and able to demonstrate your understanding
- Presented in a structure and style that suit your purpose
- Expressed clearly with accurate punctuation and spelling

Remember that it is the job of the professionals in this area to communicate effectively and efficiently. Try to do the same when you present your work.

Topic area 2
Production skills

Media communications require you to develop an understanding of many different skills. These include:

- Video and photography
- Sound production
- Publishing
- Multimedia

You are expected to choose one or more of these areas to investigate and then plan and develop these skills to show that you are developing good working practices.

Discussion

Consult with your tutor and agree the skills you need to develop and the skills you need to acqire. You should prepare for this by:

- Analysing your skills and experience
- Noting things you have done
- Noting which skills you use and when
- Identifying your strengths and weaknesses

In your discussions you should:

- Say clearly what you intend to develop and why
- Explain your intentions and use relevant technical terms
- Listen to your tutor and check you have understood; ask for clarification if anything is unclear
- Show your understanding by summarising what you have discussed

There are many opportunities for group working in this topic. This may mean you could be involved in skill swapping or skill development with others. If you are more experienced than others, you may be asked by your tutor to give a short presentation on a skill area such as:

- Using a video camera
- Making or editing a sound recording
- Using a desktop publishing package
- Developing a film and printing photographs

At level 2 you are required to give a short talk. When you give a presentation to others that involves technical advice and terms, remember to:

- Check all equipment in advance
- Give advice slowly and clearly
- Explain technical terms and acronyms
- Break down your information into points or steps
- Involve the audience; check they understand
- Use diagrams, drawings or equipment
- Allow time for audience questions
- If you don't know the answer, say so
- Offer to look things up and report back

Reading for information

Remember that no one knows everything. The range of equipment being used in media today, and the speed of innovation and development, means that everyone must constantly update their skills. You will need to:

- Read and understand technical instruction manuals for all equipment you use. These must be read in detail before operating a piece of equipment. Never guess how to use something; it could prove very costly if you are wrong.
- Research and summarise the range of skills, techniques and technologies available within your specialism. Take particular notice

of health and safety issues because you may have access to equipment and chemicals that are potentially dangerous.

Make good use of your reading time. Make notes and summarise your findings for later use.

Writing documents

You are required to:

- Create an action plan for your skill development
- Write a log of your skill development
- Keep notes on the skills you have learned
- Write up records of the feedback you receive from your tutor

Keep the following points in mind:

- The action plan should be a clear working document that sets targets and goals. You should be prepared to amend it to show how your aims and objectives change.
- The log should be kept regularly and contain a chronological record of your progress. You could use headings and sub-headings to make it easy to identify individual skills
- The notes on skill development should be clear and accessible because you will need to refer to them over time to refresh your memory on technical aspects of procedures or processes.
- The notes on the feedback should be clear because they will be used to inform changes of practice in the future.

You should include all diagrams, charts or tables that are relevant to your records; they are a valuable source of data and information; they also provide important key skill evidence.

What you must know
Part 1: The Learning Curve will help you with the knowledge you need.

What you must do
Part 2: The Bottom Line will help you with the evidence you need.

Performing Arts GNVQ

PART ONE • FOUNDATION • INTERMEDIATE

About the specifications

The Performing Arts awards study topics such as exploring opportunities in performing arts, skills development and performing work. Performance and managing arts events require a high degree of effective communication and all aspects of this skill are central to the programme of study. You will need to choose aspects that are relevant to the different topics and will give you valid key skills assessment evidence.

Topic area 1
Opportunities in performing arts

You need to build up a picture of the broad range of activities and opportunities in the industry. Your programme of study will help you to explore a variety of information sources. These will include:

Opportunities

- Primary sources such as interviews and discussions with venue managers and supervisors
- Secondary sources such as trade newspapers, the *Performing Arts Yearbook* and venue publicity

Discussion

You are expected to investigate:

- How cultural companies or venues operate
- The employment opportunities on offer.

This information can be gained through discussions with professionals who work in the industry. To conduct a good interview you need to be well prepared; here are some things to do:

- Decide in advance what you want to know about the job or venue
- Adapt your questions and your questioning to suit the interviewee
- Learn some of the key terms used by the professionals
- Prepare supplementary questions to keep your interview to the point
- Know how you will record the information you obtain

The performing arts industry is very diverse. Your programme of study may involve different people investigating different sectors and then giving a short talk to other members of the group. Level 2 requires you to give a short talk; make sure that you:

- Prepare properly and know what you're going to say
- Have notes or other aids to help you communicate
- Adapt what you say to suit your audience
- Structure what you say to help the audience understand
- If people ask, repeat or explain any terms or ideas
- Use all available resources to get your points across

Reading for information

You are expected to gain a general understanding of how the business operates by reading company reports, Arts Council publications and material from other national organisations. You should also gain a greater understanding of the range of places in which performances take place:

- Theatres, concert halls, cinemas
- Art centres and community venues, such as village halls, parks, shopping malls
- Travelling venues, e.g. circuses
- Clubs and societies

Each type of venue will have its own approach to promotion and publicity. You will be expected to collect, read and analyse a range of publicity material and other handouts to help you to see:

- How they seek to attract audiences
- The types of audience they target
- The range of outlets they use for promotion
- How a season of programmes is scheduled

Writing documents

You are not required to produce a detailed essay or report to show your depth of understanding. However, you are expected to:

- Identify how work is organised and what professionals do
- Describe the different audiences for different events and venues
- Explain how venues operate
- Use correct technical terms when you summarize your findings

You may have the opportunity to give a short talk or presentation of your findings. If so, you will need to produce short written aids to support it. If you decide to present your findings in written form, you must do four things:

- Clearly link the different parts of your findings. You could structure them around a central index and use headings and sub-headings to show when a new idea or section begins.
- Use an appropriate style of writing for different sections. Factual information should be presented simply and clearly; discussions with people in the industry could be written up to include appearances and attitudes as well as what was said.
- Use images to help you make your points. They could be maps of locations, photographs of venues or performances, and examples of promotional material.
- Be clear about your meaning and your intentions. Check your work and proof-read it. Use accurate grammar, punctuation and spelling in all finished work.

Topic area 2
Promoting, organising and evaluating events

This topic will require you to use the full range of your communication skills and work collaboratively with others as you:

- Plan, prepare and promote the event
- Manage and run the event
- Evaluate the event

You will need to find information then discuss and agree action on:

- Planning the event
  - Costs
  - Laws and licences
  - Effective advertising
  - Ticketing
  - Budgets
- Managing the event
  - Customer care
  - Health and safety issues
  - Equipment and resource hire

- Evaluating the event
  - audience feedback
  - Collecting information
  - Presenting your findings

Discussion

This is a team activity and it is important that each team member is clear about the purpose of the event and also:

- Their individual contribution within the group
- How they communicate with the rest of the group

You will have the opportunity to work on your discussion skills when you undertake your role. If you are asked to take responsibility for a particular aspect, you will have a further opportunity to provide evidence for a short talk when you brief others on the event, its purpose and organisation.

Reading for information

As part of the detailed planning for the event you will need to understand:

- The key features of the event
- How the budget will operate
- Ways of marketing the event
- Relevant laws and licences
- Health and safety practices

You will need to contribute to collecting this information by:

- Locating the relevant sources
- Skimming these sources for relevant texts
- Scanning the texts for relevant information
- Summarising the information for use by the group

Writing documents

This topic provides you with an ideal opportunity to produce written information on a variety of forms to meet a variety of purposes:

- Letters requesting information from performers or venues
- Memos to update team members on developments
- Guidelines to follow on health, safety and security
- Promotional or marketing material (posters, leaflets, tickets)
- Questionnaires for audience members to complete

You may wish to design all your documents so they have an obvious link with the event. Perhaps they could include:

- A logo or title
- A reference number
- A particular size and type of font
- A particular colour card or paper

Take great care over anything you present to the public, especially if you make a charge. Check it for accuracy in three aspects:

What you must know
Part 1: The Learning Curve will help you with the knowledge you need.

What you must do
Part 2: The Bottom Line will help you with the evidence you need.

- **Information:** have you given correct details in brochures?
- **Language:** is the grammar correct and does it make sense?
- **Spelling:** is the spelling correct, and the punctuation?

The success of your event will depend upon your ability to communicate effectively with members of your team, with your performers and with your potential audience. Used effectively, this will provide an ideal means of developing and presenting high-quality products.

Retail and Distributive Services GNVQ

PART ONE • FOUNDATION • INTERMEDIATE

About the specifications

The Retail and Distributive Services awards study topics such as investigations into the retail and distributive services sector, merchandising and display, and sales and finance.

Topic area 1
Investigating retail and distributive services

See also: **Business GNVQ**, page 114

Discussion

This topic requires you to investigate the retail and delivery services in a chosen area. It will include:

- Every type of retail outlet from the corner shop to the supermarket
- Different approaches to shopping and buying
- The distribution chain and the main methods of distribution
- The classification of different types of goods
- The legislation that applies to the sector

You will be expected to discuss them and describe them to others. This may include:

- A one-to-one session with your tutor when you provide an update on the progress you have made
- A discussion with other people on your programme when you share ideas and information on what you have found out about the chosen area
- An interview with someone who works in one of the retail outlets to find out about their job role or working conditions
- Interviews with customers when you discuss their attitudes to, and ideas on different types of shopping and the changing approaches to retail in your chosen area

At level 2 you will also have the opportunity to make a presentation of your findings to others on your programme. This could allow you to present your findings on:

Opportunities

- The types and numbers of retail outlets in your chosen area
- The range of goods available from these outlets
- The distribution services and transport used within your area
- The health and safety legislation that protects workers and customers

You will be expected to find and read, then interpret and analyse a range of printed material. This will include:

- National reports from retail and consumer organisations
- Local reports from government, councils and trade organisations
- Catalogues and brochures from high street outlets
- Publications from superstores and home shopping companies
- Maps, plans and diagrams of your chosen region or network

These diverse sources will need to be:

- Skimmed to identify what looks useful
- Scanned to pinpoint what is relevant
- Summarised to record the relevant items
- Checked for diagrams, tables and charts that help clarify information or statistics

Writing documents

You are not required to provide a detailed report of your investigations but you must produce a study. The challenge you face is to combine a range of different forms of information so that your interpretation and meaning are clear.

Use the idea of a shopping basket to create an index or structure for your findings. This structure will help readers follow and understand what you have found out:

- Provide a plan of the area showing the outlets you visited
- Describe each outlet's location; include a photo or sketch
- List the shopping basket items under appropriate headings
- Describe the distribution chain; draw a map of the network
- Include a section on the impact of health and safety legislation

Be sure that your study is clearly written, logically set out and makes accurate use of grammar, punctuation and spelling. A successful study will reveal a sophisticated and fast-moving industry and show how it aims for customer satisfaction.

Topic area 2
Buying, selling, sales and finance

The main objective of retail and distribution businesses is to distribute goods at a profit. You are expected to investigate and gather information on how an organisation:

- Buys raw materials or products
- Promotes its products and services
- Operates at the point of sale
- Finances its activity

Discussion

To gain a thorough understanding of sales administration you will need to look closely at how a business uses documentation, payment methods and security. These main documents will include:

- Purchase orders
- Invoices
- Statements of account
- Receipts
- Credit notes

You will need to discuss with others how these documents are important for financial control. This will mean that you should understand the:

- General vocabulary and expressions used in sales administration
- How to ask questions when you don't fully understand an explanation
- The vocabulary and expressions used during the explanation
- How to get more information if you need it

Opportunities may present themselves for you to pass on the results of your investigations to others by giving a short talk. As the information you are likely to present will be of a technical nature, you must:

- Be well prepared and confident in what you are saying
- Be able to explain the technical terms you use
- Have examples of any documents for the audience to see
- Break down sales administration into separate stages
- Cover each stage clearly before you move on
- Use diagrams and flow charts to illustrate the system

Reading for information

In addition to reading sales administration documents to help you understand sales and finance, you will be expected to analyse and understand copies of your chosen companies' documentation. These may include:

- Standard contract letters
- Bills of sale
- Monthly financial reports
- Annual profit and loss accounts

Spend time familiarising yourself with how each document contributes to the way your company buys, sells, pays and keeps its records. You might find it helpful to summarise your understanding of each document. Take particular note of the difference between income and profit.

Writing documents

You are required to produce the results of your investigation into the sales administration and business planning functions. These may be presented in:

- Oral form supported by notes, diagrams and handouts

What you must know
Part 1: The Learning Curve will help you with the knowledge you need.

What you must do
Part 2: The Bottom Line will help you with the evidence you need.

Opportunities

- Written form using an extended document with illustrations

Check your facts for accuracy, redraft your work until it meets your purpose and reads well, then proof-read it to pick up any spelling mistakes or similar errors.

Science GNVQ

PART ONE • FOUNDATION • INTERMEDIATE

About the specifications
The Science award studies topics such as applying practical skills in science, experimenting and carrying out scientific work, and applying scientific knowledge, skills and understanding.

See also: **Science GCSE**, page 107

Topic area 1
Measuring, observing and applying practical skills

In science the quality of your findings and conclusions and your ability to communicate them effectively to others will depend upon:

- The thoroughness of your planning
- The clarity of your purpose
- The accuracy of your observations
- The organisation of your results
- The presentation of your findings

The key skill of communication will help you to:

- Discuss your plans and preparations
- Explain your methods and results
- Read and summarise scientific sources
- Present your conclusions in an understandable form

Discussion
You will need to discuss with your tutor and others:

- Your methods, materials and equipment
- How to make measurements and observations
- How to record measurements and observations
- How many significant figures you should work to

During discussions make sure that you understand any scientific and technical language. Ask people to explain things you do not understand.

If you are working at level 2, you may be expected to give a short talk explaining your experiments, methods, processes and procedures. Some members of the audience may know a great deal about your topic and some may know nothing about it. Here is what you should do:

- Find out about your audience's level of knowledge
- Prepare properly with appropriate aids

- Check your procedures before you demonstrate an experiment
- Give clear explanations of any technical terms you use
- Describe how to work safely and follow all conventions
- Give people a chance to ask questions during your talk

Reading for information

You will be expected to read a range of textbooks and technical manuals that describe methods, health and safety issues and likely experimental outcomes. You will also be expected to read a range of instruments and take accurate measurements. Here are some of them:

- **Mass:** use spring balances (g, kg)
- **Volume:** use burettes and pipettes, (dm^3, cm^3, ml)
- **Time:** use clocks and stopwatches (h, min, s)
- **Temperature:** Use thermometers: (°C, °F, K)

Besides reading instruments, you will be expected to interpret, summarise and record information from conversion tables, charts, circuit diagrams and graphs.

Writing documents

Many of your observations, measurements and notes will be recorded in your laboratory notebook or experimental log. Use these standard conventions:

- Explain your method
- List your apparatus
- Draw relevant diagrams
- Present your measurements
- Show your calculations
- Describe chemical changes
- State results simply
- Include relevant tables
- Make your conclusions clear
- Evaluate what you've done
- Suggest future experiments

Always proof-read your writing. Check your grammar, punctuation, spelling and check any calculations.

Topic area 2
Scientific knowledge, understanding and skills

Discussion

This unit requires you to explain the principles and workings of various scientific procedures and processes. You will be expected to discuss how to explore developments in the world of science. To make an informed choice you will need to:

- Prepare your ideas and questions in advance
- Adapt your contributions to suit the situation

- Listen carefully to the advice you are given
- Ask questions to help you make your choice
- Check your understanding and look for topics to explore

At level 2 you will be expected to give a short talk or presentation on your chosen topic. This will require you to:

- Prepare notes and other aids to help you explain
- Choose language your audience will understand
- Use a structure that is easy to follow
- Use visual aids to illustrate what you say

Reading for information

You will be expected to explore a range of sources. These will include:

- Textbooks and technical manuals
- Research and commercial information
- Numerical and statistical information

The information will vary depending on the area of science you are investigating.

- Biology looks at living organisms; it monitors growth, decay, etc.
- Chemistry looks at chemicals; it monitors reaction rates, etc.
- Physics looks at machines: it measures forces, work done, etc.

Whichever area you explore and whatever sources you read, make sure you collect or summarise information in an appropriate and accessible form.

What you must know
Part 1: The Learning Curve will help you with the knowledge you need.

What you must do
Part 2: The Bottom Line will help you with the evidence you need.

Writing documents

Scientific information is very rarely presented using text only. You will be expected to communicate the information and data you have collected, effectively. This will include the use of:

- Text for methods, observations and conclusions
- Diagrams to show apparatus and results
- Numerical data from any experiments

So that other people can read and understand the results of your investigations, make sure you follow the conventions of standard written English and good science.

Index